FOR KING & EMPIRE

THE CANADIANS AT CAMBRAI AND THE CANAL DU NORD
September-October 1918

A Social History and Battlefield Tour

by N. M. Christie

CEF BOOKS
1997

Canadian Cataloguing in Publication Data
Christie, N.M.
     The Canadians at Cambrai and the Canal du Nord, September-October 1918; a social history and battlefield tour

(For King & Empire; 6)
ISBN 1-896979-18-1

1. Cambrai (France), 2nd Battle of, 1918. 2. Nord, Canal du (France), 3.Canada. Canadian Army—History—World War, 1914-18. 4. World War, 1914-18—Canada. I. Title. II. Series: Christie, N.M. For King & Empire: 6.

D545.C27C48   1997 9404'36   C97-900837-9

Published by: CEF BOOKS
                    P.O. Box 29123
                    Nepean, Ontario, K2J 4A9

Other books in this Series

Volume I: The Canadians at Ypres, 22nd-26th April 1915

Volume II: The Canadians on the Somme, September-November 1916

Volume III: The Canadians at Vimy, April 1917

Volume IV: The Canadians at Passchendaele, October-November 1917

Volume V: The Canadians at Arras and the Drocourt-Queant Line, August-September 1918

Volume VI: The Canadians at the Canal du Nord and Cambrai, September-October 1918

Volume VII: The Canadians at Amiens, August 1918

Volume VIII   The Canadians at Mount Sorrel, June 1916

Front cover picture: Canada Cemetery, Cambrai, France. Photo: N. Christie
Back cover picture: Clarence and Arnold Westcott, of Seaforth, Ontario. Clare was killed at Cambrai, September 29, 1918.

Acknowledgements: I would like to thank Clare Westcott of Scarborough, Ontario, Gary Roncetti of Port Perry, Ontario and Paul Horton of Manotick, Ontario.

Printed in Canada

This book is dedicated to

Dianne, Linda and Karen.

LOOKING DOWN THE ST. LAWRENCE

TABLE OF CONTENTS

VICTORY! November 11th, 1918

No more we weep
Dear ones, for you who sleep
 In Flemish sod.
The night is past,
And morning breaks at last,
 Revealing God.

Great is our pride
That you as patriots died
 So fearlessly.
We drained Grief's cup—
Now is Death swallowed up
 In Victory!

Norah Sheppard.

INTRODUCTION
THE BATTLE OF CAMBRAI AND THE CANAL DU NORD
September-October 1918

By 1918 the Canadians had achieved a reputation for efficiency unsurpassed in the British Army. Their success had bred a certain degree of cockiness. In March 1918 the Guards Division was holding their flank. The Canadians, showing a great disrespect for the famous Guards, dug a "defensive" switch just in case the Guards gave way. The Battle of Cambrai and the Canal du Nord was to test this Canadian confidence.

It was the last major battle fought by the Canadians in the First World War. It was also the battle in which the Canadian Corps chose to make its most complex and difficult attack. At 5:20 a.m. on September 27th, 1918, 45,000 Canadian soldiers poured across a gap 2300 metres wide, the only passable section of the Canal du Nord. The soldiers fanned out to attack German positions stretching 13,000 metres in front of them. Over the next four days they captured the Marquion and Marcoing trench systems and fought against German positions north and west of the vital transport centre of Cambrai. The 4 Divisions of the Canadian Corps battled 10 German Divisions and 13 Specialist machine-gun Companies, and still advanced. The cost was more than 18,000 Canadians killed, wounded, and missing.

By October 9th, 1918 the Germans conceded Cambrai to the Canadians and retreated. Without a rest the Canadians pursued the Germans and captured Denain, Valenciennes and on the night of November 10/11th, 1918, captured Mons; the city where the war began in August 1914.

Cambrai was the third major battle for the Canadians in 1918. At Amiens, in early August, they had driven back the Germans more than 13 kilometres in one day. Only two weeks later at Arras, the Corps broke successive lines of German trench systems, cracked the Drocourt-Queant line and turned the flank of the Hindenburg position. The victories had been costly. In the 3 major battles of 1918, the last hundred days of the war, the Canadians had suffered more than 46,000 casualties, including 12,000 dead. One fifth of all the Canadians killed in the war died in the last three months.

The Battles of Amiens, Arras and Cambrai were the greatest victories of the war for Canada. Only the capture of Vimy Ridge would equal any of these great achievements. Today, a few Canadians know of Vimy, but no one remembers the tremendous victories of 1918 or their tremendous sacrifice. The reputation of the Canadian Corps, won at such a cost and earned by the efficiency and ruthlessness of their attacks, is forgotten by their own people. War Memorials in every small Canadian town record the names of the young men who never returned. The survivors of their generation have passed into history and with them the memories of their sacrifice. But their achievements still echo in the rolling countryside of France, where in little cemeteries the men of 1918 lie buried. The fallen rest in the farmers' fields, where the sugar beet is harvested. They are rarely visited these days.

They should not be forgotten. This series of books is meant to record their exploits and pass on to a new generation of Canadians the legacy earned by their forefathers in the bloody fields of France.

The Battle of Cambrai was the last great achievement of those Canadian boys of the Canadian Corps who, during the years of the Great War, earned for Canada a reputation for excellence and courage. They left their homes to fight for their country and died in foreign fields. Perhaps Kipling best expressed it when he wrote a small poem for the unveiling of the War Memorial in Sault Ste. Marie, Ontario;

> *From little towns in a far land we came,*
> *To save our honour and a world aflame,*
> *By little towns in a far land we sleep,*
> *And trust that the world we won for you to keep!*

The Canadians of 1918 were great men and they should not be forgotten.

GETTING THERE

To be consistent with the other books in this series this guide recommends Arras as your centre of operations for visiting the Cambrai battlefields. The Battle took place 25 kilometres south-east of Arras astride the Arras-Cambrai road. The Battlefields of Arras 1918 are within 10 kilometres of Arras and the battlefield of Vimy 1917 is less than eight kilometres north. Cambrai can also be used as the centre for visiting the Cambrai Battlefields.

Arras is used to accommodating tourists and provides the best facilities in the region. Tourist authorities can provide details on bed and breakfast facilities near the battlefields for a less-expensive alternative.

Arras is the capital of the Pas-de-Calais in northern France, 170 kilometres north of Paris and easily accessible from London. A two-hour drive to Dover, a 75-minute ferry ride or a 35-minute Hovercraft journey to Calais, and a one-hour drive on the major Calais-to-Paris toll road will get you to Arras. Or you could take the rail link through the Channel Tunnel from London to Lille, which is 45 minutes north-east of Arras near the Belgian border. Arras is about 1.5 hours by road from Brussels. Check with the Tourist Board for details. Equally convenient, Cambrai is 32 kilometres south-east of Arras.

Rental cars are available in any of these cities and tourist offices can supply routes and details of hotels. In Arras, English is generally spoken in the main hotels. Otherwise, very little English is spoken. Brush up on your French before going.

In France, stores close between noon and 2:00 p.m. always. Be sure to obtain film and other necessities before closing! Stopping for a long lunch is a strict and revered tradition in continental Europe. There are 3.5 French francs (1997) to a Canadian dollar. Currency and traveller's checks can be exchanged at any bank. Always visit the Tourism Office to obtain information on accommodation or events of interest.

WHAT TO BRING

Weather is very changeable in this part of Europe. Days can start sunny and change quickly to rain, hail or even a sprinkling of snow. Above all, be prepared for wet weather.

Other than the obvious passport, traveller's checks and appropriate clothing, bring the following to ensure a successful trip:

- a bottle opener and cork screw

- binoculars

- a camera (with 100 and 200 ASA film)

- a compass

- rubber boots

- Institut geographique national map numbers 2406 east Arras, 2506 west and 2507 Croiselles 1:25,000 (they can be obtained at most bookstores in Arras)

- Michelin map No. 53 (preferably the Commonwealth War Graves Commission overprint, showing all the cemeteries)

- reference books (do your research before departure)

- a journal to record the details of your visit because you will forget.

ABOUT ARRAS

Although situated in the heart of the industrial north of France, Arras rests quietly and peacefully, with an air of grandeur and finesse reflected in its great white cobbled squares. No factory chimneys here, only the elegance of tradition which the city's inhabitants have fiercely held onto through thousands of years of captivity and terror. Badly damaged during the First World War. The inhabitants of the capital of Artois restored their incomparable monuments, the Grand'Place, the place des Héros (Petite-Place), the rue de la Taillerie and the Town Hall to their original Flemish Gothic style. This makes Arras one of the most beautiful towns in the north of France.

Of Roman origin, Arras was a stronghold in Julius Caesar's day. It was originally built on Baudimont Hill, east of the Crinchon Stream which runs through the town and called Atrebatum after a tribe which lived in the area, the Atrebates. Arras is a corruption of that name.

In the 5th century, during the reign of the Frankish king, Clovis I, Christianity was preached by Saint-Vaast, who created the diocese of Arras and was its first bishop. The most important abbey in the region was built in the 600s to honour the saint. A new town gradually emerged under the protection of this powerful monastery and was eventually separated from the original construction by a continuous line of fortifications. By the 11th century, the two communities were quite independent of each other, each with its own form of government. The older Roman city on Baudimont Hill was the Cité of Arras and was under the jurisdiction of the bishop. The other, to the west, was the Ville proper and a dependency of the St. Vaast Abbey.

While the Ville grew steadily, the Cité gradually declined until the mid-18th century when it was incorporated in the Ville. Until Arras became part of the kingdom in France in the mid-17th century, the "Ville", as the capital of the County of Artois, successively belonged to the Counts of Flanders (850-1180), the Counts of Artois (1180-1384), the Dukes of Burgundy (1384-1492) and finally to the Kings of Spain (1492-1640).

The French kings often interfered in the affairs of Arras throughout this period. The town was besieged four times by the kings of France in the 9th and 10th centuries. In the 14th century, Arras was torn by popular sedition. Under the Dukes of Burgundy, and espe-

ARRAS

2nd March. I have just returned from Arras. Oh, Lord ! What a spot! For sheer desolation I have not seen anything to equal it, and I can't describe the feeling it gives to go into it. " B.V." ought to have lived to see it before he wrote The City of Dreadful Night, but as he didn't I expect I shall have to do it for him, when next I am inspired. It's far the biggest town I have seen, in fact I suppose it is the biggest on our front, and it is just in the state that makes the horror of it most impressive, like seeing a strong healthy man dying of some disgusting wasting disease, and his limbs dropping off with scurvy. We went through a sort of Arc de Triomphe straight into one of the main streets. The street was narrow, and all the houses on either side very tall. There are no inhabitants except for men living in the cellars, and every house shows hopeless dilapidations, but almost the worst part is that the outer walls are for the most part still standing, and through the unglazed windows and the holes from the shells, you saw the broken rafters, torn bits of wall paper, the debris of bricks and furniture at the bottom. And there was the long narrow ribbon of street utterly silent, and the walls, with nothing but ruin behind them, aslant and tottering, till it seemed a push with your hand would overset them: and indeed they do collapse frequently, for we saw many heaps of bricks, and there are large notices everywhere warning you to walk close into the walls and not in the middle of the streets. You can't conceive the effect of a really big town in that state, however you try; it is far worse than seeing the place totally ruined, and in heaps of bricks and nothing more. It is those ghastly, sightless, purposeless walls that catch you, and the silence. For the life of me I could not have talked loud; I think the echo would have sent me mad.

Capt.J.E. Crombie (Gordon Highlanders).
Died of wounds received near Arras, April 23, 1917.

Destroyed house in the Petite Place of Arras.
(PUBLIC ARCHIVES OF CANADA PA-1438)

cially under Philippe-le-Bon, the town's world-renowned cloth and tapestry industries enjoyed a period of great prosperity. Its Arrazi tapestries became famous.

Arras is also infamous for imprisoning Joan of Arc during October and November 1430.

When Louis XI tried to claim Artois in 1477, the Cité of Arras promptly opened its gates to the Royal Army, but the Ville refused to surrender and was only conquered in 1479, after a long siege. Furious at the people's resistance, Louis XI exiled all the inhabitants and brought in the "Ligeriens." Arras became Spanish and its name was changed to Franchise. A few months later the people of Arras were allowed to return to their homes, and in 1483, its ancient name, armorial bearings and laws were restored.

The inhabitants of Arras resisted French domination for years following the incident with Louis XI. They opened their gates to the German and Burgundian troops of Austria in 1492, only to regret doing so when the Germans pillaged and rifled their valuables.

The Spanish-controlled city again came under the rule of the kings of France in the mid-17th century, when it fell after a long and bloody siege. The bombardments caused great damage to the abbey. A decade or so later, the town held out heroically against a Spanish invasion for 45 days.

Birth place of Augustin Robespierre, Arras was not spared during the Revolution. In 1793, Joseph Le Bon, sent there on a mission, organized the Terror. The guillotine was permanently erected in the Place de la Comédie. Travellers avoided Arras and the local merchants stopped doing business.

During the Great War, the Germans occupied Arras for only three days, September 6-9, 1914. But after their departure, the "Martyrdom of Arras" began. The Germans remained at the gates of the city until April 1917. Bombardment began October 6, 1914. Gunners fired ceaselessly on the military quarters and the two famous squares. The Hôtel de Ville, the Abbey of Saint Vaast and the Cathedral were burnt down, the belfry destroyed and by April 1917, Arras was completely in ruins. In March 1918, when the great German Offensive began, the bombardments broke out afresh. Inhabitants were evacuated and by the end of August, the British drove the enemy out for good.

A visit to Arras should begin in the architecturally-unique Grand'Place, once an orchard belonging to the Abbey of Saint Vaast, and the Petite-Place. These squares have been bordered with gabled private houses and edged with stone columns and elliptical arches supporting vaulted galleries for hundreds of years.

Merchants once drew crowds of buyers to their stalls under the porticos of the squares and the famous tapestries of Arras were once made in the damp cellars under the galleries.

Bordering the west side of the Petite-Place is the Hôtel de Ville, above which rises the graceful silhouette of the belfry. Long the centre of town, the Petite-Place attracted the townspeople to public meetings, festivals and public executions.

Today, the tourist office is located at the Hôtel de Ville (21 51 26 95) and is open daily. From there, guided tours of the underground tunnels beneath the town hall can be arranged (35 minutes, year-round). First used as cellars, the tunnels often served as shelters for the population during invasions and for the soldiers of the First World War. You can also visit the belfry.

Two-hour tours of the town are also offered by guide-lecturers of the National Association for Historical Sites and Buildings daily in July and August at 3:00 p.m. and Wednesdays and Saturdays in June and September at 3:00 p.m. Reserve at the tourist office.

The Abbey of Saint-Vaast shelters the rich collections of the Museum, and is a masterpiece of classical religious architecture.

Note, most museums in France are open 10:00 a.m. to noon and 2:00 to 6:00 p.m. and are closed on Tuesdays. Sunday and winter hours may be reduced. Abbey tel. 21 71 26 43.

Arras is famous for its "cobalt blue" porcelain, first produced in the late 18th century. It is available in most tourist shops in the town centre.

Accommodation is not a problem in Arras. You may want to check out the following hotels:

Astoria, 10 place Foch, 62000 Arras, tel. 21 71 08 14

Hôtel Ibis, place Viviani, 62000 Arras, tel. 21 23 61 61

Mercure Hôtel (3-star), 58 boulevard Carnot, 62000 Arras, tel. 21 23 88 88

Hôtel Moderne, 1 boulevard Faidherbe, 62000 Arras, tel. 21 23 39 57

Ostel des 3 Luppars, 47 Grand'Place, 62000 Arras, tel. 21 07 41 41

Hôtel de l'Univers, 5 place Croix Rouge, Arras, tel. 21 71 34 01

Some eating establishments to consider are the restaurant at the Astoria which serves traditional French cuisine, tel. 21 71 29 78; or La Faisanderie, 45 Grand'Place (opposite 3 Luppars), tel. 21 48 20 76. As well, there is a variety of restaurants and cafés at the station square.

ABOUT CAMBRAI

Cambrai is a city of 35,000 inhabitants in the Department of the Nord. It is mid-way between Brussels and Paris and 32 kms south-east of Arras. Like many of the cities in this region, Cambrai has a rich historical past. Its location on the frontiers of several empires has ensured its participation in the line of history for over two thousand years.

Cambrai's origins date back to 200-300 A.D. when it was a strategically located village used by local tribes. During the later stages of the Roman Empire the village was fortified and incorporated into the Roman defensive network designed to ward off the marauding Barbarians. Cambrai was captured by the Franks in 432 A.D.. In the 6th century the city became the religious centre for the region and prospered due to the power of the Clergy. During the Hundred Year's War the fortifications around the city were greatly strengthened. Cambrai itself was caught in the middle of the warring factions and over the next two centuries changed hands several times. In the 15th and 16th century Cambrai was under Flemish control, later in 1556, under Spanish rule and it did not come under the French sphere of influence until 1677.

The French Revolution brought a catastrophic end to the dominance of the Clergy in the city and all but 3 of Cambrai's beautiful churches were destroyed. In the following years Cambrai did not industrialize, unlike many of the other cities in the region, and it became provincial, a residence for many of the rich industrialists.

During the First World War Cambrai was occupied for 4 years, from August 1914 until liberated by the Canadians October 9th 1918. The city was devastated by the Battles around it and a conscious effort to demolish the city by the Germans prior to their evacuation in 1918. Between 1923 and 1931 the city centre was entirely rebuilt.

Cambrai was once again involved in war in 1940. German and French Armour fought a running battle north of the city in May 1940. The Germans once again occupied Cambrai until it was liberated in September 1944. Once again Cambrai had been destroyed, with more than half of all the buildings in the city damaged. This time it was not the Germans inflicting the damage but Allied bomber raids, which included many Canadian squadrons.

Cambrai is a very interesting city to visit with much fine architecture and old ruins. It welcomes tourists. The tourist office is located at 48, rue de Noyon, 59400 Cambrai (tel. 27.78.36.15.).
There are several hotels and I have listed a few possibilities below:

Le Beatus, 718, avenue de Paris, 59400 Cambrai, tel. 27.81.45.70.

Hotel de France, 37, rue de Lille, 59400 Cambrai, tel. 27.81.38.80.

Hotel de la Poste, 58, avenue de la Victoire, 59400 Cambrai, tel. 27.78.09.59.

Hotel de Ville, Cambrai.

(PHOTO: N.CHRISTIE)

Le Mouton Blanc, 33, rue Alsace Lorraine, 59400 Cambrai tel. 27.81.30.16.

La Chope, 17 rue des Docks, 59400 Cambrai, tel. 27.81.36.78.

There is a large selection of restaurants in Cambrai. A tourist will have no problem locating several fine establishments to enjoy French cuisine. At many establishments lunch is only served between 12:00 and 2:00 pm. The dinner menu will usually commence later than we are used to, often after 7:00 pm.

COMPONENTS OF THE CANADIAN EXPEDITIONARY FORCE

CAMBRAI 1918

1ST CANADIAN DIVISION

1st Infantry Brigade	2nd Infantry Brigade	3rd Infantry Brigade
1st Battalion (Western Ontario)	5th Battalion (Saskatchewan)	13th Battalion (Black Watch of Montreal)
2nd Battalion (Eastern Ontario)	7th Battalion (British Columbia)	14th Battalion (Royal Montreal Regiment)
3rd Battalion (Toronto Regiment)	8th Battalion (90th Rifles of Winnipeg)	15th Battalion (48th Highlanders of Toronto)
4th Battalion (Central Ontario)	10th Battalion (Alberta)	16th Battalion (Canadian Scottish)

2ND CANADIAN DIVISION

4th Infantry Brigade	5th Infantry Brigade	6th Infantry Brigade
18th Battalion (Western Ontario)	22nd Battalion (Canadien-français)	27th Battalion (City of Winnipeg)
19th Battalion (Central Ontario)	24th Battalion (Victoria Rifles of Montreal)	28th Battalion (Saskatchewan)
20th Battalion (Central Ontario)	25th Battalion (Nova Scotia)	29th Battalion (British Columbia)
21st Battalion (Eastern Ontario)	26th Battalion (New Brunswick)	31st Battalion (Alberta)

3RD CANADIAN DIVISION

7th Infantry Brigade	8th Infantry Brigade	9th Infantry Brigade
Royal Canadian Regiment (Nova Scotia)	1st Canadian Mounted Rifles (Saskatchewan)	43rd Battalion (Cameron Highlanders of Winnipeg)
Princess Patricia's Canadian Light Infantry (Eastern Ontario)	2nd Canadian Mounted Rifles (Central Ontario)	52nd Battalion (New Ontario)
42nd Battalion (Black Watch of Montreal)	4th Canadian Mounted Rifles (Central Ontario)	58th Battalion (Central Ontario)
49th Battalion (Alberta)	5th Canadian Mounted Rifles (Quebec)	116th Battalion (Ontario County)

4TH CANADIAN DIVISION

10th Infantry Brigade	11th Infantry Brigade	12th Infantry Brigade
44th Battalion (Manitoba)	54th Battalion (Central Ontario)	38th Battalion (Eastern Ontario)
46th Battalion (Saskatchewan)	75th Battalion (Mississauga Horse)	72nd Battalion (Seaforth Highlanders of Vancouver)
47th Battalion (Western Ontario)	87th Battalion (Grenadier Guards of Montreal)	78th Battalion (Winnipeg Grenadiers)
50th Battalion (Alberta)	102nd Battalion (Central Ontario)	85th Battalion (Nova Scotia Highlanders)

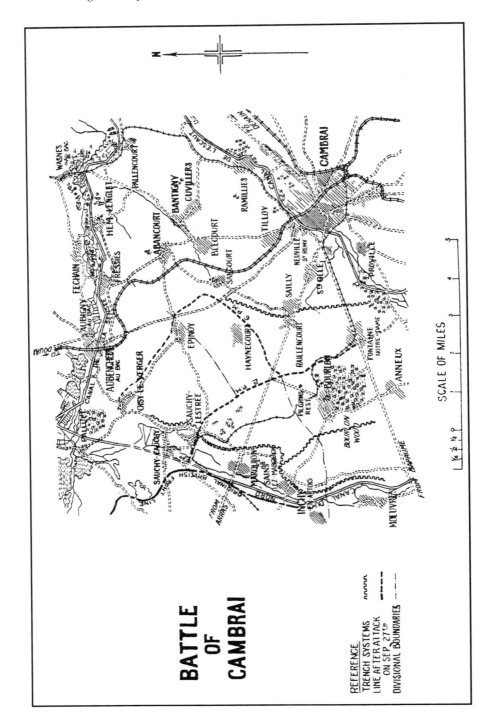

THE BATTLE OF CAMBRAI AND THE CANAL DU NORD
September to October 1918

HISTORICAL OVERVIEW

The quiet city of Cambrai first came to prominence in November 1917 when the Third British Army launched one of the most famous attacks in military history. For the first time in history a concentrated tank force was used to spearhead an attack. On November 20th, 1917, Sir Julian Byng, the General commanding the Third Army, launched his attack force of 240 tanks and 6 infantry divisions against the German's main defensive position on the Western Front, the Hindenburg line, south-west of Cambrai. Within hours the force had captured the Hindenburg position and advanced 7 kilometres, piercing the German defences as they went. The Cavalry followed their advance and for once the promised "breakthrough" was at hand.

News of the victory spread rapidly to England, where the bells chimed out the success. But all the celebration was premature for in the following days the advance was stopped and a battle of attrition began. The Germans had quickly brought in reinforcements to stymy the attack and all along the line, particularly at Bourlon Wood, had stopped the British advance.

On November 30th, 1917, the Germans delivered the cruelest stroke of all when they counter-attacked along the British line and regained virtually all their lost territory. It was a devastating blow to the morale of the British public and their Army. By December 7th the battle was over, little had changed but Cambrai went down in history as "The First Tank Battle."

The positions the British retained after the battle of Cambrai were lost in the great German offensive in March 1918. The Germans drove the British Army back to the outskirts of Arras before their offensive was finally spent.

Although the German offensives gained much territory they had not delivered the decisive blow that was required. The Germans suffered heavy casualties and were left holding weakly defended salients all along the western front. On July 18th, 1918, the French attacked north-east of Paris and won an easy victory. The second blow came at Amiens. On August 8th, 1918, the Canadian and Australian Corps smashed the German positions east of Amiens and pushed them back an incredible 14 kilometres. For the German Army the end was clearly in sight.

The Allies kept up the pressure continuously and advanced across the old Somme battlefields, capturing Bapaume and coming face-to-face with the Hindenburg line. In late August 1918 the Canadians cracked the massive German defensive lines at Arras and broke the Drocourt-Queant line. All along the front the British, Canadians, and Australians kept attacking. By mid-September the British Armies stood ready to attack the major German position from Cambrai to St. Quentin, the Hindenburg line.

The Hindenburg line ran from St. Quentin in the south, north to Havrincourt, just south of Cambrai. A northern extension ran along the banks of the Canal du Nord, west of Cambrai. This was the Canadian objective. On the night of September 26th the artillery of 3 British Armies commenced the bombardment of the German position. In the morning on September 27th, 1918 the infantry of all 3 Armies attacked. The battle continued for days.

The responsibility of the Canadian Corps was to capture the Canal du Nord line and to turn the Hindenburg position from the north. The front opposing them was formidable. The German trenches were on the eastern side of the Canal and the most of the Canal was impassable. Of the 6400 metres of the Canadian line 3800 metres were a flooded bog. Advancing across it would be impossible. However, within the Canadian sector was a stretch of 2300 metres, where the Canal bed was dry. Sir Arthur Currie, the Commander of the Canadian Corps, realized the best opportunity was to funnel his attacking divisions through the dry canal bed and then fan out and roll up the German line from the south. This plan looked very good on paper but to execute it would require perfect co-ordination of his attacking troops and most important of all, surprise. When Currie explained his plan to the former Commander of the Canadian Corps, Sir Julian Byng, Byng was impressed but concerned. "Old man do you think you can do it?" was Byng's pointed question. With less than 2 weeks to prepare, Currie put his full staff to work. His staff would have to organize the infantry attack, artillery and special Engineer units to build the bridges across the Canal and keep the men and artillery moving behind the advance.

Another major problem was how to assemble such a force so that they could keep the element of surprise. This required bringing the attacking troops close enough and hiding them in the many small woods in the area and camouflaging the guns. If they were discovered not only would the surprise be lost but a heavy enemy bombardment would inflict tremendous casualties. On the night of September 26/27th, 1918, the Corps was in place, and ready.

The defences opposing the Canadians were the northern flank of the Hindenburg line, running north to south. The first obstacle was the physical barrier of the Canal itself. It was 15 to 20 metres deep, with most of it flooded and impassable to troops. A stretch of 2300 metres was dry and passable but protected by numerous machine gun emplacements. Directly east of the Canal was the Canal du Nord trench system, 2 kilometres beyond it was the Marquion trench system, protected by the imposing height of the Bourlon Wood. East of the Wood, between it and Cambrai, was the third and final German trench system, the Marcoing line. Added to this defensive capability were a series of fortified shell holes protected with barbed wire. The Germans had also fortified the houses and villages just east of Cambrai. The trench lines could be attacked with traditional methods, but the other defences would have to be eliminated one by one. Most of the German defences were new and many had yet to be discovered by the Intelligence staff. They were to be found the hard way, in battle.

September 27th, 1918

Currie's plan was to attack with his favourite troops, the 1st and 4th Divisions. Two battalions of each Division would have the honour of leading the attack. The 44th (Manitoba) and 46th (Saskatchewan) Battalions would lead the attack across the dry Canal bed, attack due east and capture the Canal du Nord trench line. The 50th (Alberta) Battalion would continue the advance and capture the Marquion line. Other battalions of the 4th Division; the 38th (Eastern Ontario), 85th (Nova Scotia Highlanders), 87th (Grenadier Guards of Montreal) and the 102nd (Central Ontario) would continue the advance and capture Bourlon village, and the critically important position of Bourlon Wood. The balance of the 4th Division battalion would be employed as required to advance east of Bourlon

THE FIRST TANK BATTLE
Cambrai 1917

1917 had been a bleak year for the Allies. It had a promising start in April with the initial success of the Battle of Arras, but after April 9th, 1917 it was all downhill. The later stages of the battle had floundered with heavy losses, the French offensive had failed and resulted in mutiny. Russia had surrendered, the Bolsheviks took power, Italy had been hammered at Caporetto and the Battle of Passchendaele had cost hundreds of thousands of casualties with very little gain. The morale of the Allies was at its lowest point of the War.

But failure had produced one positive change. Sir Julian Byng, the former Commander of the Canadian Corps, was placed in Command of the British 3rd Army. Byng was an unusual man, results-oriented and open to new ideas. His 3rd Army had not been involved in any major attacks since May 1917, it was fresh and ready.

Byng had developed a modern concept for the First World War. He proposed using the modern innovation of the tanks, used in mass formation, in an area where the ground conditions were right and he would attack a specific strategic target. In addition he would employ the element of surprise. There would be no massive preliminary bombardment to warn the Germans. His 3rd Army would create the breakthrough which the cavalry would exploit to its fullest capability. Whether or not the disasters of 1917 had weakened the obstinacy of his superiors, somehow Byng gained approval for his project.

His strategic target was Cambrai, a vital supply centre for the Germans. The 3rd Army would capture the canal crossings south of the city, Bourlon Wood and the Arras-Cambrai road, the heights west of Cambrai and cut-off the German Divisions on the Arras front. To achieve his victory Byng employed 240 tanks of the Tank Corps and 6 infantry Divisions, some trained to operate in cooperation with the tanks. The ground chosen was good, and this part of the Hindenburg line was known the be weakly held. Byng also

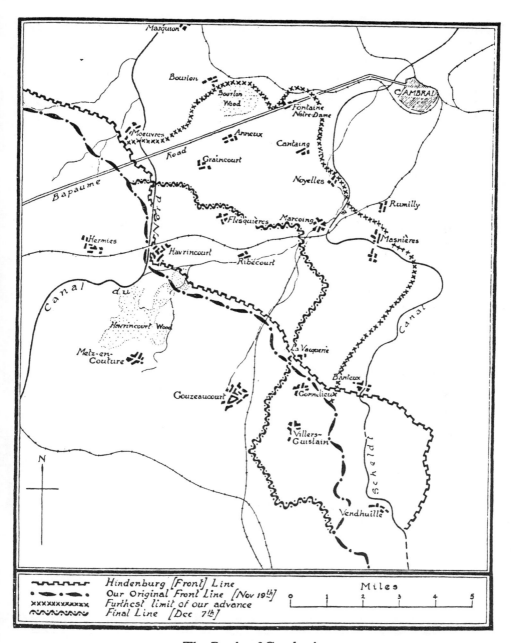

The Battle of Cambrai

knew he had only 2 days to exploit any success before masses of German reinforcements would arrive.

On the morning of November 20th, 1917 a new era in Warfare was born. Byng's troops quickly overran the Hindenburg line, advancing 7 kilometres. His cavalry advanced to the Scheldt Canal, south of Cambrai. One squadron of the Fort Gary Horse got across the canal and Lieutenant Harcus Strachan attacked and captured an enemy battery. Strachan was awarded the Victoria Cross[1].

The attack south of Cambrai had gone well but the attacks west of Cambrai had encountered some difficulty and they were not advancing on schedule. German resistance at Bourlon Wood was especially problematic and no advance could be made against this fortified position.

The successes of the first day were enough to set bells ringing all across Britain. The breakthrough was at hand. The next few days saw heavy fighting west of Cambrai. The Germans fought tenaciously and the impetus of the initial attack had waned.

On November 23rd the British continued their attacks on Bourlon Wood, but all failed. By the 28th and 29th the offensive was spent. The Germans had held and on the morning on November 30th, 1917 they launched a major counter-attack and, after 7 days of fighting, regained the majority of their original positions. The Battle closed on December 7th, 1917. It had cost the British 44,000 killed, wounded and missing for no territorial gain. Cambrai launched a new era in Warfare but it's lessons would not be utilized until the Second World War.

The initial euphoria of the battle turned into anger and Byng was scrutinized for his tactics at Cambrai. It had been a "cruel disappointment."

---

[1] Born at West Lothian, Scotland; died at Vancouver, British Columbia, May 1st, 1982.

and capture the Marcoing line. The plan was very ambitious.

The 1st Division was assigned the task of fanning out to the north, capturing the villages of Sains-les-Marquoin and Marquion, advancing across the Arras-Cambrai road and capturing German positions in front of the Marcoing line. The 4th (Central Ontario) and 14th (Royal Montreal Regiment) would make the initial assault and the 13th (Black Watch of Montreal) and the 1st (Western Ontario) would pass through and capture the Marquion line. The next phase would be left to the 15th (48th Highlanders of Toronto) to capture Marquion. The 5th (Saskatchewan), 8th (Black Devils of Winnipeg) and the 10th (Alberta) would carry the attack across the Arras-Cambrai road and drive in a north-easterly direction towards the Marcoing line. The British 11th Division would cover the left flank of the 1st Division. The 3rd Division was to be used to attack the German defences on the outskirts of Cambrai. The 2nd Division was held in reserve.

At 5:20 a.m. on September 27th, 1918 the attack commenced. The Germans were surprised by the attack and the assaulting battalions were quickly across the Canal and into the German positions. The attack by the 46th and 44th was successful but as the other battalions attacked, they came under heavy machine gun fire from the exposed southern flank. The advance continued and as the 102nd pushed south of Bourlon Wood they suffered heavily from German machine guns. Lieutenant Graham Lyall, of the 102nd Battalion was awarded the Victoria Cross for leading his company forward and capturing 185 prisoners, 26 machine guns and one field gun, over two days! By 10 a.m. the 38th, 85th and 87th Battalions had captured Bourlon village and pushed north around the wood towards the Marcoing line. The 78th (Winnipeg Grenadiers), 72nd (Seaforth Highlanders of Vancouver), and the 54th (Central Ontario) Battalions carried the attack east of Bourlon Wood and by 7 p.m. halted their advance west of the Marcoing line. Lieutenant Samuel Honey, of the 78th Battalion, single-handedly captured a German machine gun that was holding up the advance. He later captured 3 more machine guns. Honey was mortally wounded on September 29th, 1918. He was awarded the Victoria Cross posthumously.

The 1st Division attack went smoothly and they had quickly captured Sains-les-Marquion, the Marquion line and Marquion. As was typical of the 1st Division throughout the war they executed per-

*Canadian transport move across the dry bed of the Canal du Nord. A dead
Canadian lies in the foreground.*
(PUBLIC ARCHIVES OF CANADA - PA-3285)

fectly and were an unstoppable formation. Lieutenant George Kerr, of
the 3rd Battalion, was awarded the Victoria Cross for leading his
men across the Arras-Cambrai Road, rushing and capturing machine
guns (and 31 prisoners) which were holding up the advance. By the
end of the day the 5th and 10th Battalions had captured Haynecourt
and were within striking distance of the Marcoing line. They had
advanced so quickly it would be 3 days before the other Divisions
caught up to them.

The plan for September 28th was to capture the Marcoing line,
west of Cambrai. To do this Currie employed the 3rd Division and
elements of the 4th Division. The 1st Division would wait for their
comrades to bring up their flank before attacking.

Problems at this point of the attack were several fold. The enemy
defences in this area were not totally understood by the attacking
Canadians. The Germans' defence protecting Cambrai was not
always trench positions. They employed many specialist machine gun
companies who would set up in shell holes or slit trenches and would
have to be dealt with one by one by the advancing infantry, as artillery

would have little effect on them. Secondly, the Germans had put up many belts of barbed wire and these obstacles were not always shown on the trench maps used by the Canadian officers. The Canadians also knew Cambrai was of vital importance to the Germans and they would not let it go easily. German reinforcements were already arriving to stem the Canadian advance. The 3rd Division relieved the 4th Division east of Bourlon Wood and on the morning of September 28th the men of the 3rd Division opened their assault on the Marcoing line. Going was hard for the 43rd (Cameron Highlanders of Winnipeg). Their objective was to capture Fontaine-Notre Dame, a village from which the Germans fired into the flank of the Canadian attack. They succeeded. The 52nd (Northern Ontario), and 58th (Central Ontario) Battalions attacked and broke into the Marcoing line. The 116th (Ontario County) Battalion attacked towards St.Olle and Cambrai. They suffered heavily from German machine gun fire.

The Royal Canadian Regiment and the Princess Patricia's Canadian Light Infantry attacked the Marcoing line at Raillencourt and Sailly. The fighting was fierce but the R.C.R.s fought courageously and broke through. The day's action won a Victoria Cross for Lieutenant Milton Gregg of the R.C.R.s. Gregg crawled through the uncut barbed wire until he found a gap and led his men forward. He then returned across fire-swept ground to get more hand grenades for his men. The P.P.C.L.I. continued the attack in a northeasterly direction and were successful until they ran into barbed wire entanglements, blocking their advance across the Cambrai-Douai road. They were forced to withdraw. In the action their Commanding Officer, Charlie Stewart, an original member of the Regiment from 1914, was killed. The 50th and 47th (Western Ontario) Battalions of the 4th Division attacked on the left of the 3rd Division and broke through the Marcoing line north of Raillencourt. By nightfall most of the Marcoing line had been captured but the ad hoc German defences and the performance of the Specialist machine gun Companies had taken a serious toll on the Canadian attacks. The attackers were exhausted and their ranks depleted by casualties.

Currie was aware his Corps were in a fight for their lives. His plan offered no possibilities for withdrawal or respite, so on the 29th he threw his weakened Divisions once again at the German defenders.

September 29th was a day of confusion, but elements of the 3rd and 4th Divisions attacked along the Cambrai-Douai road, north-west

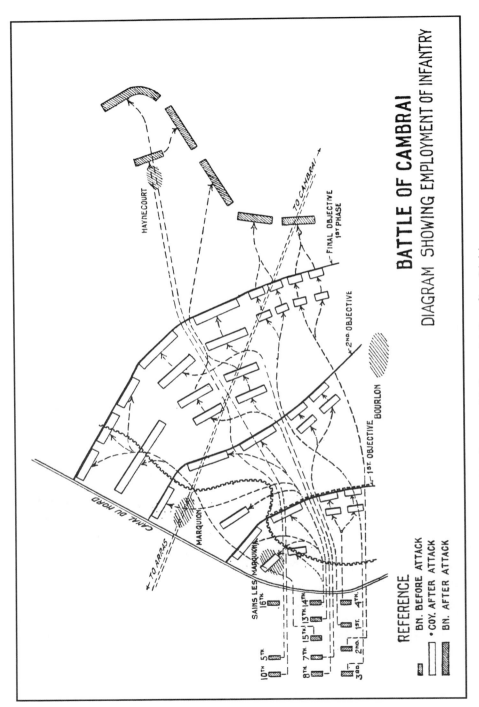

Employment of Infantry, 1st Canadian Division

of Cambrai and in brave actions against machine guns and uncut barbed wire, the men advanced. The 116th Battalion continued their attack on St. Olle and Cambrai. The 1st (Saskatchewan) and 2nd (Central Ontario) Canadian Mounted Rifle Battalions attacked the western suburbs of Cambrai and suffered heavy casualties. Captain John McGregor, of the 2nd C.M.R., was awarded the Victoria Cross for knocking out machine gun posts and leading his men under the heaviest of fire. The P.P.C.L.I., R.C.R.and the 49th (Edmonton) of the 3rd Division and the 75th (Mississauga Horse) and the 72nd Battalions of the 4th Division attacked against German positions along the Cambrai-Douai road. For heavy casualties, few gains were made. Only the 72nd Battalion succeeded in breaking through and capturing Sancourt village.

On September 30th Currie again threw his depleted battalions against the Germans. Miraculously, the Canadians captured Tilloy village and Tilloy Hill but were always under heavy fire and their positions were tenuous.

A Canadian soldier hides behind a tree to avoid sniper fire. A comrade lies dead in the ditch to his right.

(PUBLIC ARCHIVES OF CANADA - PA-3266)

In a final attempt to crack Cambrai, the attack was renewed on October 1st, 1918. This time Currie had the 1st Division attack the Marcoing line north of Sancourt. The 1st (Western Ontario) and the 4th (Central Ontario) Battalions advanced towards Abancourt but against heavy machine gun fire from the railway embankment in front of Abancourt and with an exposed flank, they could not achieve their goals. Sergeant William Merrifield, of the 4th Battalion won the Victoria Cross. He single-handedly knocked out 2 machine gun posts near Abancourt.

South of that attack the 13th, 14th and 16th (Western Canadian Scottish) Battalions were initially successful, capturing the villages east of Sancourt; Blecourt, Bantigny and Cuvillers. But with the failure of the 1st and 4th Battalions' attacks to the north, they were heavily enfiladed, and counter-attacked and forced to evacuate all three villages. It was the only defeat the 1st Division had since 1915! South of the 1st Division, the 102nd and 87th Battalions of the 4th Division successfully pushed east, carefully watching their exposed flank. Four battalions of the 3rd Division covered the southern flank.

The Canadian Corps was exhausted. It had encountered 10 German Divisions and 13 Specialist Machine gun companies. Having advanced against these odds, they could advance no further.

The British attacks on the southern Hindenburg line continued and by early October the Third British Army cracked the German defences south of Cambrai.

On October 8/9th, 1918 the 4th (Central Ontario) and 5th (Quebec) C.M.R. Battalions forced the bridges across the Canal into Cambrai. In this action, Captain Norman Mitchell of the Canadian Engineers, was awarded the Victoria Cross for under heavy fire, cutting the demolition wires of an explosive charge placed by the Germans on the bridge over the Canal de l'Escaut. He then captured 12 prisoners and held his bridgehead until relieved.

Other than the rearguard, the Germans had gone. The Battle of Cambrai was over.

The 2nd Division pursued the German rearguard and fought at Iwuy on October 9-11th, 1918 and after that it was a chase. The Canadian Corps pursued the Germans, captured Denain and fought their last set piece battle of the war on November 1st, 1918, in the Capture of Valenciennes.

Arthur Currie was the most capable Soldier Canada has ever produced. Through his successes as the Commander of the Canadian Corps, Currie rose to international prominence beyond what has been achieved by any Canadian before or since. He was born in Strathroy, Ontario, December 5th, 1875. As an adult, he moved to British Columbia where he became involved in Real Estate. Like all good Canadian businessmen he joined the Canadian Militia and became the Commander of the 50th Gordon Highlanders Militia. He joined the Canadian Expeditionary Force in 1914, and fought with exceptional coolness at Ypres in 1915, where his 2nd Brigade made an incredible stand. Having impressed his Superiors, Currie was promoted to command the "crack" 1st Canadian Division. He led the "Red Patch" at Mount Sorrel, the Somme and in its classic success at Vimy. In June 1917 Currie succeeded Julian Byng as Commander of the Canadian Corps. Over the next 17 months Currie's Canadians won several decisive victories, but it is for his classic victories at Amiens, Arras and Cambrai he is best known. The breaking of the Drocourt-Queant line is considered the greatest Allied victory of the war. Arthur Currie was tall and overweight with a typically Canadian ability to use course language, which certainly upset his British Superiors. He was also open-minded, pragmatic and careful with others' lives, rare qualities in a First World War General. But it was his ability to organize, plan and execute which set him apart from all others. Currie could always "deliver the goods." He returned to Canada in 1919 with little fanfare and later became the Principal of McGill University. Arthur Currie died in 1933. His funeral was a major event in Montreal and thousands lined the streets to honour the Great Leader of the Canadian Corps. He is buried in Mount Royal Cemetery.

General Sir Arthur Currie. Commander of the Canadian Corps, 1917-19.
(PUBLIC ARCHIVES OF CANADA - PA-1370)

On the night of November 10/11th, 1918 the 42nd (Black Watch of Montreal) and the R.C.R. captured Mons. At 10:58 a.m. on November 11th, 1918 Private George Lawrence Price of the 28th (Northwest) Battalion was killed by a sniper east of Mons. He was the last Canadian killed in the war. At 11:00 a.m., November 11th, 1918 the Great War ended.

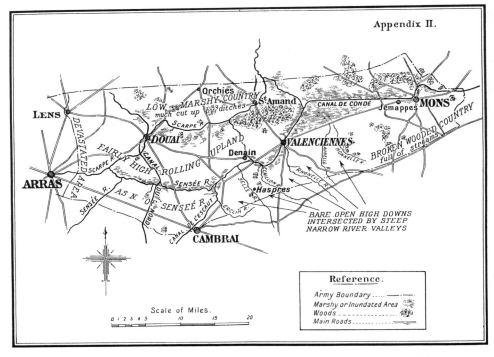

The Advance to Victory by the Canadian Corps. August to November 1918.

TOUR ITINERARY:
Duration 5 hours

Point 1:   Crossing the Canal du Nord at Inchy.

Point 2:   Ontario Cemetery, the advance of the 4th Division.

Point 3:   Quarry Cemetery, the advance of the 1st Division.

Point 4:   Crest Cemetery, the Marcoing line.

Point 5:   Drummond Cemetery, the Marcoing at Raillencourt.

Point 6:   Sancourt British Cemetery, the attack of the 1st and 4th Battalions.

Point 7:   Canada Cemetery, the fighting north of Cambrai.

Point 8:   The Grande Place of Cambrai.

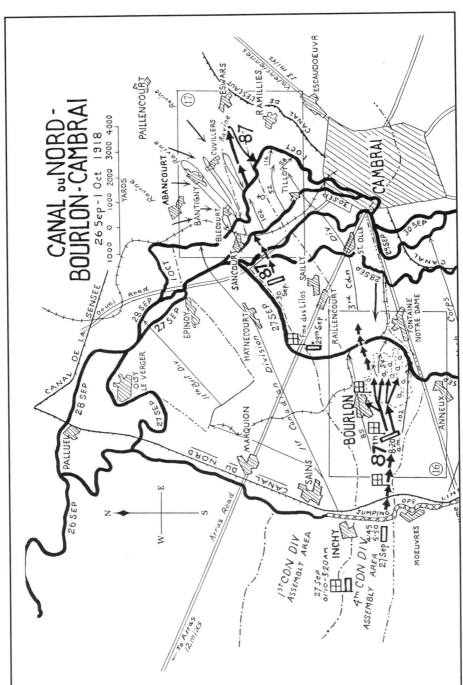

The attack on the Canal du Nord and Cambrai.

THE BATTLE OF CAMBRAI 1918

THE TOUR

This tour starts from the centre of Arras. Follow the road signs to Cambrai on the D939. You will exit Arras through the south-east of the city. Follow the D939 for 22 kilometres, past the villages of Tilloy-les-Mofflaines, Vis-en-Artois, and Dury (pass the Dury Canadian Battlefield Monument on your left). You are traversing the Battlefields of Arras 1917 (from Tilloy to Monchy-le-Preux) and the Canadian Battle of Arras 1918 and the Breaking of the Drocourt-Queant line (from Tilloy to Dury). The Battle of Arras 1918 was the greatest Canadian victory of the War and it cost Canada 16,000 dead and wounded. The Drocourt-Queant line crossed the D939 just west of the Canadian Dury Monument (see for King & Empire Volume V: The Canadians at Arras 1918).

Turn right 3.5 km past the Canadian Monument at Dury, on the D14, into the village of Barralle and take the D19 (to the right) to Inchy-En-Artois.

This is the area where the 45,000 men of the Canadian Corps assembled, awaiting the attack on September 27th, 1918. The area was extremely congested and a severe German bombardment, particularly one using gas, could have inflicted heavy casualties. Fortunately, the Germans never realized the situation. Once in the village follow the D22 north-east out of the village. After 750 metres you arrive at the Canal du Nord bridge crossing. Just before the bridge pull over on the drive-by and stop your car.

Point 1: Crossing the Canal du Nord at Inchy en Artois.

It was at this point, between Moeuvres (the village to the south) and where you stand, that the Canadian Corps launched their attack on the 27th September 1918. Two battalions each of the 1st and 4th Divisions crossed the canal here as the canal bed was dry. The attack was dependent on these 4 battalions quickly driving across the canal, securing sufficient space for the support battalions to fan out and roll up the flank of the German trench systems protecting the Canal-du-Nord. Where you stand, the 4th (Central Ontario) Battalion attacked. North of the 4th, the 14th (Royal Montreal Regiment) attacked across the canal and into Sains-Les-Marquion. To the south of you the 46th (South Saskatchewan) and 44th (Manitoba) forced

By Snaffles

" THE CANUCK "

their way across the canal and pushed east toward the Marquion Line and Bourlon Wood. Bourlon Wood can be seen on the horizon (the large wood on the ridge) and was the objective of the 4th Division that day. The Canadians jumped off at 5:20 a.m. and caught the Germans by surprise. The Germans recovered and against heavy artillery barrage and machine gun fire the Canadians advanced. The 44th Battalion advanced too quickly and were caught by their own bombardment. Several officers and N.C.O.'s were killed trying to bring the men back. Immediately following the capture of the canal, the Canadian Engineers went to work bridging the canal. Support troops crossed quickly, awaiting their turn to pass through the attacking troops and follow-up the attack.

Return to your car and continue. After 800 metres, you hit D15. Turn right and drive 700 metres until you come to Ontario Cemetery. Stop at the cemetery.

Point 2: Ontario Cemetery, the advance of the 4th Division.

Looking east from the cemetery you can see the ground over which the Canadians advanced. To the south you can see Quarry Wood and on the eastern perimeter of the wood, Quarry Wood Cemetery, which contains the graves of 263 Canadians of the 4th Division, killed in the advance. The 50th (Calgary) and 44th (Manitoba) attacked across the fields and many men of these units, killed in the attack, are buried in the cemetery.

Looking north is the village of Sains-Les-Marquion and to the east of the village the field of advance for the fanning-out attack of the 1st Division can be seen. The 13th (Black Watch of Montreal) and the 1st (Western Ontario) attacked over that area. The success of the 1st Division was remarkable. Their initial objectives were gained and quickly followed-up. The 1st Division drove through the Marquion Line where it crossed the Arras-Cambrai road, capturing Marquion Village and turned north-east to Haynecourt. By the end of the day they had reached the Marcoing Line east of Haynecourt (it is the Air Force Station north of the Arras-Cambrai road, but is beyond your view from this Point).

Looking west towards the canal you see where the initial battalions crossed the dry bed of the canal.

Return to your car and turn around and drive on the D15 to Sains-les-Marquion. You will pass Sains-les-Marquion British Cemetery. This cemetery is almost completely Canadian and contains the graves of many 1st Division men killed in the north-easterly attacks, particularly men of the 3rd (Toronto Regiment) and the 7th (British Columbia) Battalions are buried here.

Continue on the D15 until the eastern outskirts of Marquion are reached after 1.7 km. Turn right when Quarry Cemetery is signposted. Stop at the cemetery. Walk through the cemetery to the small triangular park south of it.

Point 3 Quarry Cemetery, the advance of the 1st Division.

From this position in the cemetery looking south and south-east you view the attacks of the 4th Division at Quarry Wood and the second phase of the attack as the 4th Division passed through to attack the Marquion line in front of Bourlon village.

The 7th (British Columbia) Battalion attacked through the position where you now stand. To the north, the 13th (Black Watch of Montreal) and the 15th (48th Highlanders of Toronto) attacked and captured Marquion village, and the Marquion line, where it crossed the Arras-Cambrai road.

To the east, the imposing feature of Bourlon Wood is visible on the horizon. The closer you get the more dangerous this position appears. It is easy to understand its importance in the Battle of Cambrai, 1917, when the Germans stopped the British advance in the wood.

The cemetery is very beautifully designed and located. It contains many 1st Division men killed in the village of Marquion and the battlefield to the east.

Return to your car and drive back to the fork of this minor road (Chemin de Bourlon). Take the south fork to Bourlon village. In the 3 km distance to Bourlon village you are crossing the battlefields of both the 1st and 4th Divisions. After 0.5 km you reach the position where the Marquion Line trench system cut the road, and the area of attack of the 3rd Battalion. During this action Lieutenant George Fraser Kerr[2] won the Victoria Cross. The attack was held

---

[2] George Fraser Kerr, VC, MC & Bar, MM. Born at Deseronto, Ontario June 8, 1894; died Toronto, December 8, 1929.

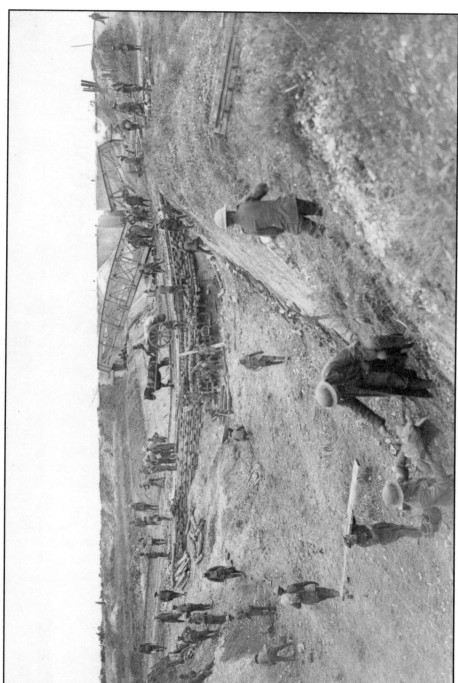

Canadian transport move across the makeshift bridges constructed in the dry bed of the Canal du Nord.

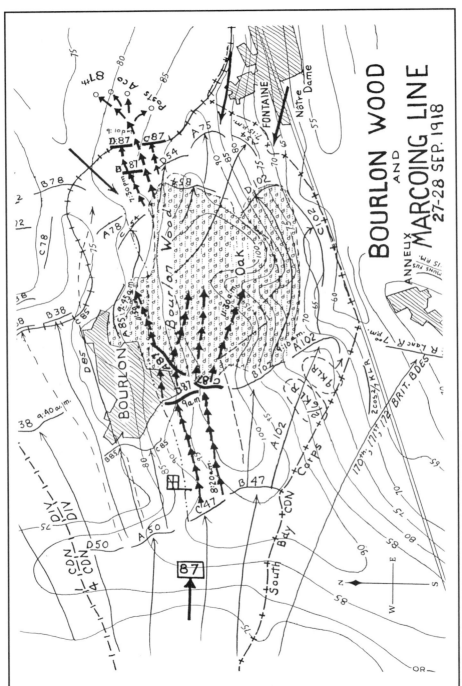

The 4th Division's attack on Bourlon.

up by heavy machine gun fire and Kerr led an outflanking move, silencing the gun. He later rushed a strong point single-handedly and captured 4 machine guns and 31 prisoners.

As you approach the village you cross the field of attack of the 2nd (Eastern Ontario). The attack of the 72nd (Seaforth Highlanders of Vancouver) Battalion was just to the east. The 72nd swept north of Bourlon village and the wood. Once in the village (captured by the 85th (Nova Scotia Highlanders) Battalion), follow the sign posts to the Bourlon Canadian Memorial. The memorial is worth a quick visit but is situated in a wood and visibility is poor. It is also worthwhile to visit Bourlon Wood Cemetery, in the woods north of the memorial. It contains mostly 4th Division men.

Return to your car and drive back through the village keeping left on the main road and continue out of the north end of the village.

Once you clear the village you are again in the midst of the Canadian attack. The 78th (Winnipeg Grenadiers), 2nd and 3rd Battalions attacked across this road from the south to the north. It was across these fields that Lieutenant Samuel Honey[3], DCM, MM, won his Victoria Cross. Throughout September 27th-28th, Honey led assaults against stubborn and deadly German machine gun positions. He captured many guns and prisoners. On one occasion he went out on a night raid by himself and captured a machine gun position! Samuel Honey was mortally wounded on September 29th, and died at Queant the next day.

Once the Arras-Cambrai road (D939) is reached turn right towards Cambrai. The village north of the Arras-Cambrai road is Haynecourt and was captured by the 1st Division on 27th September, 1918. The 5th (Saskatchewan) Battalion captured Haynecourt village. The region east of the village was captured by the 10th (Alberta) Battalion on the 27th September 1918. They halted their assault within attacking distance of the Marcoing line. There they waited for the 4th Division to catch up.

Drive 2.5 km to Raillencourt. To the south Bourlon is clearly visible.

---

[3] Samuel Lewis Honey, VC, DCM, MM. Born at Conn, Ontario February 5, 1894; died of wounds at Queant, France September 30, 1918.

The Action of the 44th Battalion (Manitoba) at the Canal du Nord, September 27th 1918. (From their official history).

As the last minutes tick off before zero, long lines of infantry form up in the dim light. Zero by the 44th watches! For a second or two there is no sound. Watchers on the ridge look back anxiously toward the silent battery positions. Suddenly the gaunt trees on the Baralle-Inchy Road spring into sharp relief against a sheet of flame - the combined flashes of opening guns. Storms of bursting shrapnel hide the Canal positions in front. Increasing in intensity as the heavy siege guns come into action against the enemy rear positions, the roar of the barrage swells into a vast pulsating crescendo of sound like the thunder of a mighty cataract.

Starting up with the first gun, the waves of the 44th men advance. Driving forward, close under the wall of bursting shrapnel, the forward line blots out the enemy post line in front of the Canal and, with scarce pause, keeps steadily on. The barrage rests for a few minutes on the Canal line. As the line of the Canal du Nord lies at an angle of some 35 degrees from the line of the Tenth Brigade front, the barrage to the left clears the Canal some time before it does on the 44th front. Seeing the troops on their left climbing over the Canal locks, the men of the leading 44th platoons run forward - into the barrage. Many keen, brave men are thus cut down by their own gunfire. A swiftly passing glimpse of heroism will live in the memories of survivors who see officers and NCO's rush forward into the line of bursting shells, in an effort to hold their men back.

Lieut. Wilkins is hit as he vainly tries to save the lives of his forward sections. Lieut. Cronin, standing with arms outstretched in the barrage, is spattered from head to foot with the explosion of an incendiary shell and stands like a living cross outlined in blazing phosphorus. Lieut. Flook, "old original" stretcher bearer who has just returned to the unit from Bexhill, is killed - as are Sergt. Curry, Sergt. J. Mills, Sergt. J.T. Millroy and many other NCO's - trying to hold back the leading waves. All four Company Commanders are wounded before reaching the 44th objective. The intensity of the barrage is appalling - utterly drowning the steady beat of the enemy machine gun fire. Despite the number of the 44th casualties from machine gun fire there are men who afterward insist that not a German machine gun came into action.

Soon the guns lift to positions beyond the Canal. The attacking waves surge up and over the massive walls. Ladders are placed and men in the leading sections reach down to help their comrades. The speed with which the assaulting Companies sweep through the Canal defences seems little short of miraculous. So rapid is the attack that the German garrison, crowded in the Canal shelters, has little time to offer resistance. Hundreds of prisoners fall to the attacking Companies. In one dugout alone, over 150 men of the 4th Ulanen are captured. But the 44th men drive straight ahead, losing no time in any attempt to collect or send back prisoners.

As the 44th men pass over the farther Canal wall, they encounter strong resistance. Machine gun fire from the right sweeps the platoons in enfilade. Casualties are frightful. But the men press on and are on the top of the German garrison in a sunken road and the supporting trench system, close behind the barrage. Once across the Canal, the Battalion fans out; and before reaching its objective, the Companies are in the front line of attack - due to the gaps on the right.

A sunken road, 600 yards beyond the Canal, is the 44th objective. It is reached exactly on schedule time. The German defence makes a desperate effort to check the attack but, fighting gallantly, is over-powered. The 47th platoons following close behind, sweep through the 44th lines while the fighting is still in progress and press on toward the crest of the hill, where the dark shadow of Bourlon Wood loom sin the growing light. Away to the left, men of the First Division are seen fighting hard to gain ground against the German reserves beyond Quarry Wood. Back at the Canal, Canadian Engineers work like madmen. Obstructions are cleared - crossings constructed and, in an incredibly short time, tanks are rolling across the Canal to the support of the First Division.

Bourlon Village, October 1918.

(PUBLIC ARCHIVES OF CANADA - PA 3332)

THE BOURLON WOOD CANADIAN MEMORIAL

The Canadian monument at Bourlon Wood, west of the City of Cambrai, stands on one of eight First World War Canadian battlefields officially commemorated.

In 1920, the Canadian Battlefield Monument Commission decided to erect memorials at:

St. Julien - to commemorate the Second Battle of Ypres
Hill 62 - to commemorate the Battle of Mount Sorrel
Courcelette - to commemorate the Battle of the Somme
Vimy - to commemorate the Battle of Vimy Ridge
Passchendaele - to commemorate the Battle of Passchendaele
Le Quesnel - to commemorate the Battle of Amiens
Dury - to commemorate the Battle of Arras 1918 and the capture of the Drocourt-Queant line
Bourlon Wood - to commemorate the Battles of the Canal du Nord, Cambrai, the capture of Valenciennes and Mons and the March to the Rhine

It was decided that Vimy would act as the National Memorial and have a unique design. The other seven would be marked with identical memorials. A competition was held to choose an architect to design the monuments. Walter Allward of Toronto was chosen for Vimy's unique memorial and Frederick C. Clemesha of Regina took second place. Clemesha's design, "The Brooding Soldier," was built at St. Julien and had such a stark effect, at its unveiling in 1923 that the Monument Commission decided it also should remain unique.

In conjunction with the architectural advisor, P. E. Nobbs, the cube design was developed for the remaining six monuments. A 13 tonne block of Stanstead granite was used for each. A wreath was carved into two sides of the monument and on the other two sides was engraved a brief explanation of the exploits of the Canadian Corps in that specific battle. One side is in English, the other in French.

At Dury, the monument reads:

THE CANADIAN CORPS ON 27TH SEPT. 1918 FORCED THE CANAL DU NORD AND CAPTURED THIS HILL. THEY TOOK CAMBRAI, DENAIN, VALENCIENNES AND MONS: THEN MARCHED TO THE RHINE WITH THE VICTORIOUS ALLIES.

Around the base of the stone, it reads:

HONOUR TO CANADIANS WHO ON THE FIELDS OF FLANDERS AND OF FRANCE FOUGHT IN THE CAUSE OF THE ALLIES WITH SACRIFICE AND DEVOTION

The land on which this Memorial has been erected was donated to the Canadian Government by Count de Francqueville of Bourlon. It marks an historic and brilliant attack by the Canadian Corps that contributed to the rapid demise of the German Army. The tragic cost, with only 42 days remaining in the war, was more than 18,000 Canadian dead, wounded and missing.

The Bourlon Wood Canadian Memorial, circa 1928

By the end of the day, 27th September, 1918 the Canadians had advanced east of Bourlon Wood and Haynecourt. The Germans recovered on the 28th September 1918 and the next few days would involve some of the heaviest fighting of the war. The Germans had reinforced the Marcoing line and added specialist machine gun companies to their defences.

When Raillencourt is reached turn right on the D140, at the sign post for Crest Cemetery (and Fontaine Notre-Dame). The cemetery is 1 km south of the village in open ground. Stop at Crest Cemetery.

Point 4: Crest Cemetery, the Marcoing line.

Crest Cemetery is located 1 km west of the Marcoing Line. The Marcoing Line ran north-south from Raillencourt-St.Olle, to Fontaine Notre-Dame and was the last major German trench system in front of Cambrai.

Looking east you can see where the Marcoing Line crossed the fields and the villages on the eastern edge of Cambrai; Raillencourt, Sailly, St.Olle, and the main buildings of Cambrai. To the north-east, the village of Tilloy and heights beyond it, are visible. It was to be the scene of heavy fighting on the 29th and 30th.

Looking west, you can see Bourlon Wood and the territory captured by the Canadians on 27th September 1918. It was south of the wood that Lieutenant Graham Lyall[4], of the 102nd Battalion, led a small group of his men against a German strong point. He single-handedly rushed the Germans, killed the officer in charge and captured 47 prisoners. Lyall courageously led his men on with similar success. By the end of the 28th he had captured 185 prisoners, 26 machine guns and one field piece! Not surprisingly Lyall was awarded the Victoria Cross.

The attack on the Marcoing Line started from here, on the 28th September 1918 with the plan of driving through the Marcoing Line and capturing the well-defended villages in front of Cambrai.

The freshly-arrived 3rd Division was to spearhead the assault. They would attack in the triangle between the Arras-Cambrai and Bapaume-Cambrai roads against the Marcoing Line. The Royal

---

[4] Graham Thomson Lyall, VC. Born at Manchester, England March 8, 1892; killed in action in North Africa November 28, 1941.

Canadian Regiment would attack south of Raillencourt. The 43rd (Cameron Highlanders of Winnipeg) were to capture Fontaine-Notre-Dame. The attack by the 43rd Battalion was critical for the Canadians. It should have been captured the day before by a British Division. They failed and the flank of the Canadians had been subjected to heavy enfilade fire. On the 28th September, 1918 the 43rd attacked over the rise to the south and captured Fontaine-Notre-Dame. The 47th (Western Ontario), of the 4th Division, attacked Raillencourt.

The attack was launched at 6:00 a.m. and encountered great difficulty with uncut barbed wire and heavy machine gun fire. The 52nd (Northern Ontario), 58th (Central Ontario), 49th (Edmonton), 116th (Ontario County) and the Princess Patricia's Canadian Light Infantry also attacked in the confined triangle.

Due east of where you stand, the Royal Canadian Regiment captured the front trench of the Marcoing Line but ran into difficulties with the support trench system. To their right the 52nd ran into difficulty on the high ground to your right. On the extreme right, and over the rise, the 43rd Battalion captured Fontaine-Notre-Dame.

The P.P.C.L.I. came to the aid of the R.C.R. and by noon of the 28th September, both units had pierced the Marcoing Line.

The P.P.C.L.I. continued on the attack in a north-east direction behind Raillencourt. They ran into heavy wire and stiff resistance from the Germans. The breaking of the Marcoing Line was a success but the attempt to exploit the gains towards Cambrai ran into problems from the fortified houses and slit trench machine gun emplacements. The Germans had no intention of losing Cambrai.

After breaking the line, the 116th and 58th (Central Ontario) drove east towards Cambrai, but met heavy resistance from St. Olle. On the 29th, the 116th continued their attack and suffered more than 300 dead, wounded and missing; their worst day of the war.

The 3rd Division had advanced and by the evening of the 28th had penetrated the Marcoing Line. The gains for the day were reasonable but the casualties were heavy. Amongst the dead was Lt. Col. Charlie Stewart, Commanding Officer of the P.P.C.L.I. He

The grave of Charlie Stewart, Ontario Cemetery, Sains-les-Marquion, France.

Charlie Stewart was one of the original characters of the Princess Patricia's Canadian Light Infantry. He joined the unit in August 1914 and served with it throughout the war, rising from Lieutenant to Commanding Officer. During the Battle of Cambrai, near the Marcoing line "Stewart was hit in the spine and in the back by a bursting shell falling behind him and died almost at once." He was known to all as a Ladies' man and someone who loved the high life, even if it was beyond his means, but in the trenches he was a strong leader. Charlie Stewart was 44.

was the third C.O. of the P.P.C.L.I. killed in the war. Stewart was killed by an enemy shell about 200 metres north of Crest Cemetery and is buried in Ontario Cemetery, Plot I, Row D, Grave 2.

On the northern flank, along the Arras-Cambrai road, the 4th Division was also able to enter the Marcoing Line and take the small villages of Raillencourt and Sailly and drive north-east into Sancourt village.

The going was tough. For 29th September 1918 the strategy would remain the same. Keep the pressure on. Sooner or later the Germans would crack. However, after the heavy fighting of August and September 1918 and knowing the ferocity with which the Germans would defend Cambrai, who would crack first?

Return to your car and drive back to Raillencourt. Turn right on the D939 to Cambrai. The Marcoing Line crossed the D939 between Raillencourt and Sailly-Les-Cambrai at Raillencourt Communal Cemetery, which appears on your right.

Continue 2 km to St. Olle and watch for the signpost to Drummond Cemetery, which will appear on your left, near the Water Tower. Turn left to Drummond Cemetery, it is located one kilometre off the road. Drive to the cemetery and stop.

Point 5 Drummond Cemetery, the Marcoing line at Raillencourt

From Drummond Cemetery you see the battlefields of the final 4 days of the battle.

Looking north-east you can see the high ground of Tilloy Hill (Mont Blanc to the French) and Tilloy village. It would be the scene of heavy fighting on the 30th September. Before reaching Tilloy, the 3rd Canadian Division would have to breach an unchartered defensive position along the Cambrai-Douai road (N43). The N43 runs in a north-west direction, 1 km north-east of where you stand.

Picking up from Point 4; after breaking into the Marcoing Line on the 28th September the P.P.C.L.I. advanced rapidly to exploit their success. They advanced quickly until surprised by belts of uncut barbed wire on the west side of the Cambrai-Douai Road. Their regimental history noted that the attack was a failure, for the same reasons as in so many previous battles: infantry cannot advance against uncut wire. The P.P.C.L.I. and the 49th (Edmonton) Battalions found this out all too well and were forced to withdraw. The Royal Canadian Regiment also met similar difficulties in the wire and it was along

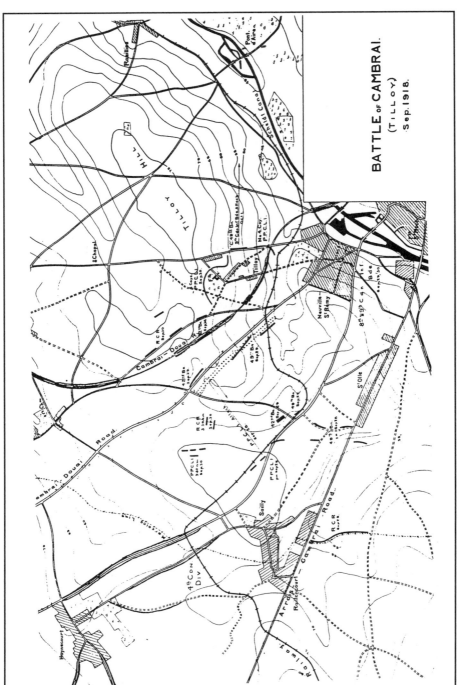

Third Division attacks along the Cambrai-Douai Road and Tilloy.

Attack of the P.P.C.L.I. on the German Position along the Cambrai-Douai road. (From their official history).

There is little to say of the Regiment's first attack on the Douai road and railway except that it failed. The Divisional General's report, concerned with the achievements of the battle as a whole and emphasizing the partial revenge of September 30, leaves this abortive attempt to inference. But the failure is easily explained; the facts are set out in the battalion report, and the very bluntness of statement makes them more tragic, though assuredly not inglorious. The barrage seemed at first to be "most effective," but it was undoubtedly incomplete, for General Clark reports that "enemy bombing planes working very heavily and accurately are interfering with batteries firing my barrage." The Patricias attacked behind the barrage, with Nos. 2 and 3 Companies in the front line and 1 and 4 in support. At first all went well. The Regiment swept forward some 2000 yards north-eastwards up the track to the Douai road with such ease that the embankment objective seemed well within its powers. Numbers of prisoners were captured form the 207th and First Guards Reserve Divisions; and there was every indication that the Patricias were "going strong." Then they ran into wire. Along the south-west side of the Douai road were stretched two belts of uncut wire. These were not shown upon any map, and, personal reconnaissance being impossible, the obstacle was entirely unforeseen.

The Patricias now learned the grim lesson taught in blood to so many a fine battalion before, that infantry caught in wire are helpless against machine guns. Nos. 2, 3 and 4 Companies were raked by the guns which commanded them from the railway and Tilloy Hill and enfiladed them from the south. There was a single obvious gap in the wire and every one made a dash for it; but this proved to be a trap, for the German guns were trained upon the spot and mowed down the men as they tried to rush through. Every desperate effort to find a way through failed, and the three companies, terribly mauled, were forced back some distance behind the road. No. 1 Company found another gap, rushed the road, and pushed on almost to the railway. There it was completely isolated, and Captain MacBrayne, as senior officer in the line of attack, gave the word to withdraw behind a large engineers' dump and saw-mill on the Douai road. At 10.35 p.m. this officer reported to Captain Edgar:

We are not in touch with the 49th and have just located the 44th [the 4th Division unit attacking on the left] about 600 yards on my left rear. Have sent out officer and one other rank to reconnoitre, and shall in all probability have to get in touch with 44th by retiring. Have no stretchers. Line I am holding at present merely dug in and not much of a defensive position. No. 1 Company alongside Douai - Cambrai road, which has several lines of wire and has trenches camouflaged and good fighting positions for the enemy.

the Cambrai-Douai road that Lieutenant Milton Gregg[5] won the R.C.R.'s only Victoria Cross of the war. This action took place at the N43, just before and after the Motorway overpass to the north-east (the attack north of the overpass will be discussed in Point 7). Gregg crawled through the wire and found a narrow gap through which his men could pass. He then led an attack on the German position, killed machine gun crews and captured 48 prisoners. His heroic action captured half of the German defensives in front of the R.C.R.s.

The real objective of the attack had been Tilloy Hill and the railway line running generally north-south in front of it. So, as the objective was not attained, the attack was renewed on the 29th September 1918. The 42nd (Black Watch of Montreal) and the 49th Battalions attacked, against the uncut wire on the Cambrai-Douai road, from the overpass to 600 metres south along the road. The 49th's attack failed and although the 42nd suffered they found a path through the wire and managed to advance.

Although not visible from here, the 4th Division was suffering similarly, against the German positions along the Cambrai-Douai road and the railway embankment east of it. At the same time on the 29th September, the 1st (Saskatchewan) and the 2nd (Central Ontario) Mounted Rifles pushed across the open fields into the outskirts of Cambrai. The advance was slow and costly. The 1st C.M.R. suffered heavily in the field between you and St. Olle (to the south) from severe enfilade fire from the village. This little village lent itself well to the German defence and from it the Germans devastated the 116th and the 1st C.M.R. on 28th-29th September, 1918. The dead of these Battalions are buried here at Drummond Cemetery, St. Olle British Cemetery (south of the D939) and Raillencourt Communal Cemetery. Tilloy Hill and village were captured on the 30th September by the P.P.C.L.I. but by this time many of the battalions were depleted. Many of the attacking battalions had suffered as many as 500 killed, wounded and missing and were down to company strength.

The 3rd Division was kept in the line and asked to attack in conjunction with a main thrust to encircle Cambrai by the relatively healthy 1st Division and an equally exhausted 4th Division.

---

[5] Milton Fowler Gregg, VC,CBE,MC & bar. Born at Mountain Dale, New Brunswick April 10, 1892; died in New Brunswick March 13, 1978. Served as Minister of Fisheries 1947-48 and Minister of Veteran's Affairs 1948-50.

Two men of the 75th Battalion with their prisoner near Raillencourt, October 1918.

Return to your car and drive back to the D939 turn right towards Arras. Pass through St. Olle and turn right into Sailly-lez-Cambrai. Follow the road (D140) through the village towards Sancourt, continue past Cantimpre Canadian Cemetery (the cemetery contains many graves of the men of the 4th Canadian Division killed on the 28th-29th September, 1918. The 75th (Mississauga Horse) suffered heavily in their attack and 48 of their number are buried there). Cross the N43 to Sancourt village. You are driving across the fields captured by the 4th Division on 28th September, 1918. The village was captured by the 72nd Battalion on 28th September, 1918. Follow the sign to Sancourt British Cemetery. It will take you down a sunken, cobblestone road into open fields. Stop at the cemetery.

Point 6: Sancourt British Cemetery, the attack of the 1st and 4th Battalions.

The 1st Canadian Division had stopped in front of the northern sector of the Marcoing Line on September 27th, and waited for the other Divisions to catch up to protect their flank. They had seen very

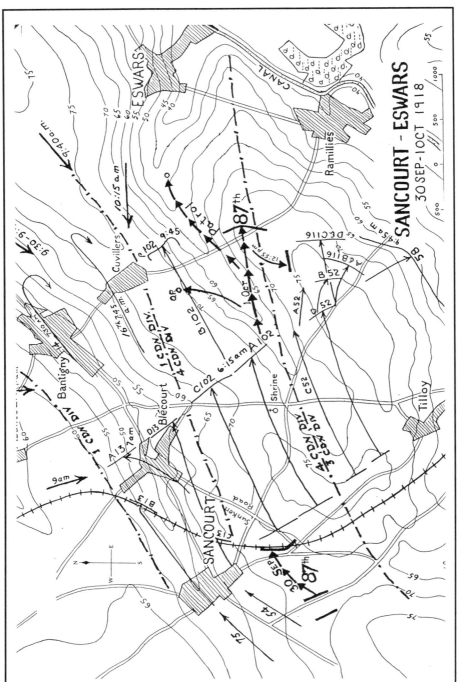

The attacks North-West of Cambrai

little action since the 27th, but were called to attack with the 4th and 3rd Divisions on 1st October, 1918.

The Marcoing Line ran in a north-west direction, virtually through the cemetery where you now stand. A strong second line was made along the railway embankment 1.2 km east of the cemetery. The railway position ran north from Cambrai, east of Sancourt and west of Abancourt (the village north-east of you). The flat terrain gave a great advantage to the German defenders, who by this time contained several battalions of "crack" German machine gun troops. At 5:00 a.m. on 1st October 1918 the 1st Division attacked. The 1st (Western Ontario) and 4th (Central Ontario) battalions attacked through the field in which you stand. Both units advanced towards Abancourt and had some initial success. However the British Division on their left had failed to keep up with the Canadian attack and as a result they were devastated by the German machine gunners in the railway embankment. Finally, after heavy losses, they dug-in in front of the railway. Bravery sustained the attack under devastating fire. One such action was that of Sergeant William Merrifield[6], of the 4th Battalion. He attacked 2 machine gun positions, which were pouring devastating fire on his men, by rushing from shell hole to shell hole until close enough to kill the Germans. Merrifield was wounded after silencing the first position but continued on to destroy the second. His bravery was acknowledged by the award of the Victoria Cross. The attack was a failure and many of the men of the 1st and 4th Battalions are buried in Sancourt British Cemetery. Sancourt village had been captured on the 29th September by the 72nd (Seaforth Highlanders of Vancouver). On the 1st October the 13th (Black Watch of Montreal), the 14th (Royal Montreal Regiment) and the 16th (Western Canadian Scottish) Battalions attacked from the posts established by the 72nd. The focus of the attack was the 3 small villages due east from where you stand. Success was immediate, if unexpected. They captured Blecourt, then Bantigny and Cuvillers. These villages are clumped due east of the cemetery. Blecourt is the first you see. By noon it became apparent the Germans were not through. They heavily counter-attacked the battalions and the Canadians were forced to make a fighting retreat. All of the three captured villages

---

[6] William Merrifield, VC,MM. Born at Brentwood, England October 9,1890; died Toronto August 8, 1943.

The Action of the 16th Battalion at Blecourt, on October 1st, 1918.
(From their official history).

The whole area was swept with machine-gun fire; sniping was very bad. I took three runners and , well spread out, we went forward circling to the right. This route brought us to the Blecourt chapel road at the chapel - a six-sided shrine with small windows on each side. From here through my field glasses I had a splendid view of the whole country. Enemy movement was visible in the outskirts of Blecourt, on my extreme left, and at Cuvillers in front. The road from the chapel to Blecourt is partly sunken and our men coming from the forward area found shelter in this section of it.

Quite a number of the 4th Division came back to this cover, including three officers who told me that they had been beyond Cuvillers and had run into our own barrage. We decided to make the road a rallying point and began digging in, the 16th on the left of the chapel lining the road towards Blecourt, the 4th Division men on the right of the chapel. By this time heavy fire was brought to bear upon us from Cuvillers, where the enemy could be seen coming out form the houses carrying machine guns.

The position of the men in front of this road - small groups of 14th and 16th in shell-holes under no proper control - was very unsatisfactory, so we got them back as soon as possible. During this reorganization, Regimental Sergeant-major Kay did splendid work. A strong counter-attack was threatened; the ammunition situation was desperate. Kay moved up and down amongst the men encouraging them and ordered them to reserve their ammunition until the enemy came close up; then to let them 'have it,' and attack with the bayonet. The effect of Kay's cool, determined leadership was most inspiring.

Cover was fair up to the cross roads but from there to the entrance of the village the road was swept with machine-gun fire from the tower of the Blecourt church. Sniping from the houses in the village was also very bad. We, therefore, formed another line of defence, echeloned in rear of the left flank of our front line; the balance of the 16th mingled with the 14th were placed in this position in gun pits and shell-holes and other places where cover was available.

On our extreme left about one hundred and fifty yards from the Blecourt church, which was situated near the south-east end of the village, I came on one of our orderly room runners high up on the embankment. He hailed me to jump into his small trench. He was busy, all on his own, trying to get the snipers in the church tower, who were bothering our men so much. We could easily see them at the windows and observed them duck when fragments were broken off the wall from this man's shots. Returning, I told our nearest Lewis gun section to keep in touch with this lone sniper.

were lost and the Canadians were virtually back to their jump-off line. For the 1st Division, the most successful of all the Canadian Divisions, 1st October 1918 was a disaster. The 16th (Western Canadian Scottish) suffered 82 dead, 194 wounded and 69 prisoners. The number of prisoners exceeded those captured in the Gas Attack at Ypres in April 1915.

Not visible from the cemetery was the action of the 4th and 3rd Divisions attacking along the railway embankment further south.

Return to your car (if the road is good) continue north for 1.4 km to the D21E and turn right to Abancourt. To your right is the battlefield of 1st October 1918. After 1.5 km you cross the railway (no embankment any more) which caused so many Canadian deaths. Drive through Abancourt and turn right on the D402 to Blecourt, continue through the crossroads following the D49 to Cambrai. You see many sunken roads and why the Germans defended this area so effectively. After 2 kilometres turn right when you see the sign for Canada Cemetery. Stop at the cemetery. The territory you have just crossed was captured by the 3rd and 4th Divisions on 1st October, 1918.

Point 7: Canada Cemetery, the fighting north of Cambrai.

At this point we are viewing the battlefields of the 3rd and 4th Divisions of 29th-30th September to 1st October 1918.

Looking west along the embankment of the motorway you can see (south of the large factory) Mill Switch Cemetery on a bank overlooking the Cambrai-Douai road (N43). This was the northern part of the battle which took place in front of the uncut barbed wire, west of the N43, discussed at Point 5. It was at Mill Switch the P.P.C.L.I. and the 42nd were cut down. Just north of that cemetery, blocked by the factory, are the fields the 4th Division heroically attacked on the 30th September - 1st October 1918 suffering heavy losses, particularly the 75th Battalion.

On 1st October the 102nd (Central Ontario) and 87th (Grenadier Guards of Montreal) captured the fields you stand on. They drove east past Canada Cemetery capturing the land as far as Cuvillers village (north-east of you) and the fields 2 km east of you. They maintained their gains whereas the 1st Division had been forced to withdraw in the north.

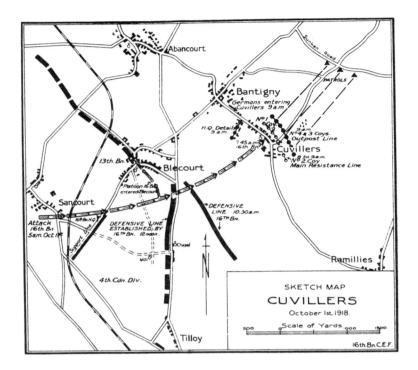

The embankment of the motorway to the south blocks the view of Tilloy Hill and village. On 30th September 1918 the P.P.C.L.I. had captured the village and on 1st October 1918, the 43rd (Cameron Highlanders of Winnipeg), 52nd, 58th and the 116th Battalions successfully attacked Tilloy Hill but were unable to close on the Canal l'Escaut (on the north side of Cambrai). The number of attacking battalions was deceptive as most were reduced to less than half strength, many down to less than 200 men, the size of one company!

Return to your car and drive back to the D49. Turn right to Cambrai. After you go over the motorway Tilloy Hill appears on your left and the village on your right. Both were the scene of heavy fighting.

After 2 km you cross the Canal de l'Escaut. On 1st October the 1st and 2nd Canadian Mounted Rifles reached the canal but were unable to cross it. The German fire was intense and any movement would receive an immediate response. Captain Jack

McGregor[7], of the 2nd C.M.R., led his men, although wounded, against the German guns. He single-handedly, in broad daylight, put the German crews out of action. McGregor remained in the line in spite of his wounds and greatly aided in the advance north of Cambrai. Captain Jack McGregor was awarded the Victoria Cross.

The positions remained unchanged until pressure supplied by the Canadians and the Third British Army to the south forced the Germans to evacuate Cambrai on 9th October 1918. Continue into Cambrai following the signs to the Centre Ville. When you reach the Grande Place stop.

Point 8 The Grande Place of Cambrai.

On 9th October 1918 the Germans set fire to Cambrai and abandoned it. The 4th (Central Ontario) and 5th (Quebec) Canadian Mounted Rifles pushed across the Canal de l'Escaut and captured the evacuated city. For the Canadians the battle was over but the pursuit of a shaken enemy was about to begin. On 9th-10th October 1918 the 2nd Canadian Division pushed against the Germans north-east of Cambrai and drove them back. On the 11th October 1918 the 2nd Division attacked towards the village of Iwuy, 7 kms north-east of Cambrai. The 20th (Central Ontario), 21st (Eastern Ontario), 31st (Alberta) and 27th (City of Winnipeg) attacked successfully and drove back the Germans. But even in successful battles there were many dead. Most of these killed in action at Iwuy are buried in Niagara Cemetery, 1 km south of Iwuy. Amongst the dead buried there is Lieutenant Walter Lloyd Algie[8], VC, of the 20th, killed while leading his men against German machine guns south of Iwuy. They captured the machine guns and forced the Germans to evacuate Iwuy. For his bravery Algie was posthumously awarded the Victoria Cross.

In one month the war would be over but the soldiers in the line did not know this. So, for the men there was no rest, pressure had to be maintained. At this point, although disorganized, the Germans were still fighting well and the Canadian losses at Cambrai testify to this. The Canadian Corps would pursue the Germans to the very end and capture Denain and Valenciennes. They could never let the

---

[7] John (Jack) McGregor, VC,MC & bar,DCM. Born at Nairn, Scotland February 1,1889; died at Powell River, British Columbia June 9,1952.

[8] Wallace Llloyd Algie, VC. Born at Alton, Ontario June 10, 1891; killed in action at Iwuy, France October 11, 1918.

Canadian soldiers in Cambrai, October 9, 1918.

Germans have a moment to construct effective defences. The pursuit continued until 11th November 1918 when Mons was liberated by the 3rd Canadian Division. On this, the last day of the War, the last Canadian soldier to die, Private George Lawrence Price, of the 28th (Saskatchewan) Battalion, was killed by a sniper at 10:58 a.m. Two minutes later it was all over.

Have a coffee in Cambrai and maybe reflect on the sacrifices of those Canadians two generations ago. I think amidst the sadness for young lives lost will be a certain and strong pride in being Canadian. The cost to Canada for the Battle of Cambrai 1918 and the Canal du Nord was 18,000 killed, wounded and missing.

Return to Arras on the D939. It is well signposted in the city. Arras is 32 kilometres from Cambrai.

On your way back, along the D939, the Arras-Cambrai, you will traverse the battlefields of Cambrai, Canal du Nord, Drocourt-Queant and the Fresnes-Rouvroy Line. In less than six weeks in 1918, more than 9,000 Canadians died along it, and another 27,000 were wounded.

When war was declared in 1914 Major Louis Lipsett, of the Royal Irish Regiment, was attached to the Canadian Militia in Winnipeg. He joined the Canadian Expeditionary Force as the Lieutenant Colonel of the 8th Battalion, Little Black Devils. The Irish-born Lipsett, led the 8th in their incredible stand at Ypres in 1915 and was later promoted to command the 2nd Canadian Infantry Brigade. After the death of Major General Malcolm Mercer at Mount Sorrel in June 1916, he took over the 3rd Canadian Division, which he led with distinction at The Somme, Vimy, Passchendaele, Amiens and Arras. With the war coming to an end, and with no prospects for continuing his career with the Canadians, he transferred to the 4th British Division in September, 1918. He had been one of the great leaders of the Canadian Corps and greatly contributed to its success. On October 14th, 1918, "Lipsett was killed by a sniper while crawling out under fire to find out for himself the exact situation. He refused to let his Brigadier go out with him. The latter saw him hit, crawled out to him, asked him if he could make a run for a wood about 100 yards off. He had been shot in the jaw very badly. He said he could. They made a run for it but on reaching the wood he lay down and died almost at once." On October 15th, Louis Lipsett was laid to rest at Queant Communal Cemetery, in the presence of the Prince of Wales, Horne,(the 1st Army Commander) and Arthur Currie (the Canadian Corps Commander). Each battalion of the 3rd Division supplied a 100 men Honour party. The Honour Guard was supplied by the 8th Battalion, who fired the final salute. Louis Lipsett, C.B., C.M.G. was 44.

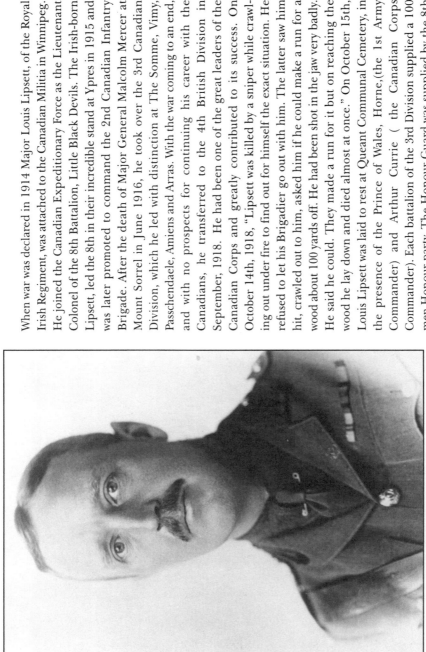

Major-General Louis Lipsett.
(PUBLIC ARCHIVES OF CANADA - PA 7442)

CEMETERIES AND MEMORIALS OF THE BATTLE OF THE CANAL-DU-NORD AND CAMBRAI
September - October 1918

Canadian cemeteries dot the fields between Arras and Cambrai. The majority were left as they were made in 1918 by the Canadian Corps Burial Officers. They have been landscaped and the crosses replaced by headstones but the locations have not changed and from the locations a great deal can be understood of the battle. The Battles of 1918 were successful and therefore over 90% of the soldiers who died have a known grave, unlike the battles of Ypres 1915 or Passchendaele 1917 where the vast majority lay in unknown graves or remain beneath the farmers fields.

The small original cemeteries which mark the battles are rarely visited today. Off the beaten track of the tour companies' itinerary of Ypres or the Somme, they never receive the attention they deserve.

QUEANT COMMUNAL CEMETERY EXTENSION

The cemetery is located on the north-west outskirts of Queant village which is 20 kms south-east of Arras. The cemetery was made by fighting units and field ambulances in September-October 1918. Although located at the southern end of the Drocourt-Queant line, captured on 2nd September 1918 all burials relate to the battle of the Canal du Nord and Cambrai. It contains the graves of 276 Commonwealth soldiers of which 112 are Canadian.

Buried in Row C Grave 6 is Lieutenant Samuel Lewis Honey, VC, DCM of the 78th Battalion (Winnipeg Grenadiers). Honey was awarded his Victoria Cross for several acts of bravery between 27th-29th September 1918. He was wounded on the 29th and died on the 30th. He was the son of the Reverend George and Metta Honey of Lynden, Ontario. Honey was 24 years old.

Major General Louis Lipsett, CB, CMG, Commander of the 4th British Infantry Division is buried in Row F Grave 1. Lipsett had been with the Canadians from August 1914 until September 1918. He had commanded with tremendous skill the 8th Battalion (90th Rifles of Winnipeg) at Ypres 1915, the 2nd Canadian Infantry Brigade in 1916 and the 3rd Canadian Division from June 1916 to Sept. 1918.

He was an outstanding performer for Canada and his loss was deeply felt by all those who served with him.

TRIANGLE CEMETERY, Inchy-en-Artois

This beautiful, little cemetery is located south-east of the village of Inchy-en-Artois, 25 kms south-east of Arras, on the road to Cambrai.

It was made by fighting units and field ambulances. It contains the graves of 90 Commonwealth soldiers of which 69 are Canadian (2 are unidentified). The graves are predominantly men of the 4th Canadian Division.

ONTARIO CEMETERY, Sains-les-Marquion

The cemetery is located south of Sains-les-Marquion, across the Canal du Nord from Inchy. It was made by fighting units and enlarged by battlefield clearances after the war.

It now contains the graves of 341 Commonwealth soldiers of which 145 are Canadian (3 are unidentified). They are predominantly 1st Division.

Amongst those buried here is Lieutenant Colonel Charlie Stewart, DSO and bar, of the Princess Patricia Canadian Light Infantry. Stewart was the third commander of the P.P.C.L.I. killed in the war. He was an original member of the "Pats." He was killed near Sailly-les-Cambrai on the 28th September 1918. He was 44. Buried beside him are 5 officers of the P.P.C.L.I. killed in the same action (Plot I, Row D).

Six officers of the 42nd Battalion (Black Watch of Montreal) and 1 of the 49th Battalion (Edmonton Regiment) killed 28th-29th September 1918 are buried in Plot II Row C. The bodies were brought back to the Canal from Cambrai for burial.

Captain Eric Davis, MC of the 4th Battalion (Central Ontario), killed 27th September 1918, is buried in Plot I Row A Grave 1. Davis' acrimonious relationship with a fellow officer (and later author) Lieutenant J.H. Pedley, MC is well documented in Pedley's excellent book, *"Only This."*

QUARRY WOOD CEMETERY, Sains-les-Marquion

The cemetery is located 1 km south of Ontario Cemetery, down a track leading to Quarry Wood. The cemetery was made by the 102nd Canadian Battalion in October 1918.

It contains the graves of 277 Commonwealth soldiers of which 263 are Canadian (3 are unidentified). The burials are virtually all 4th Division killed in the initial assault across the Canal-du-Nord and the advance on Quarry Wood.

Of the 263 Canadians buried in the cemetery 33 were decorated. Two of them, Lieutenant Arthur Kilburn, DSO, MC, MM, of the 78th Winnipeg Grenadiers and Private Oliver Swire, DCM, MM and bar of the 44th (Manitoba) Battalion, were decorated 3 times.

SAINS-LES-MARQUION BRITISH CEMETERY

The cemetery is located south of the village, which is 25 kms southeast of Arras; south of the Arras-Cambrai road.

The cemetery was made by the 3rd Canadian Infantry Brigade in September 1918. After the war it was enlarged by battlefield clearance which brought in 61 graves.

It contains the graves of 255 Commonwealth soldiers of which 185 are Canadian (8 are unidentified). The burials are predominantly 1st Division killed in the northern flanking movement, rolling-up the Canal du Nord line at Sains-les-Marquion and Marquion. It was a highly successful operation.

QUARRY CEMETERY, Marquion

The cemetery is located east of the village of Marquion which is 25 kms south-east of Arras; south of the main Arras-Cambrai road. It was made by fighting units in September-October 1918.

It contains the graves of 68 Commonwealth soldiers of which 45 are Canadian. The burials are those of the 1st Canadian Division killed near Marquion.

BOURLON WOOD CEMETERY, Bourlon

The cemetery is located in Bourlon Wood north-east of the Canadian Battlefield Memorial. It was made by the Canadian Corps Burial Officer in October 1918.

It contains the graves of 245 Commonwealth soldiers of which 226 are Canadian (5 are unidentified). The burials reflect the fighting of the 4th Division at the Marquion line and in Bourlon.

ANNEUX BRITISH CEMETERY

The cemetery is located 6 kms south-west of Cambrai on the road to Bapaume. It was made from battlefield clearances after the war and contains many unknowns of the Battle of Cambrai 1917.

It now contains the graves of 1013 Commonwealth soldiers including 86 Canadian (7 are unidentified). The Canadian burials reflect the actions of the 3rd and 4th Division's attack on the Marcoing line at Fontaine-Notre Dame.

CREST CEMETERY, Raillencourt

The cemetery is located in open fields south of Raillencourt, which is 3 km north-west of Cambrai on the Arras-Cambrai road. It was made by the Canadian Corps Burial Officer in October 1918.

It contains the graves of 88 Commonwealth soldiers of which 87 are Canadian (5 are unidentified). The burials reflect the actions of the 3rd Division against the Marcoing line between Fontaine and Raillencourt on the 28th September 1918.

This spectacular, little cemetery reflects the ethic diversity of the Canadian Corps. Among the 82 identified Canadian burials are men who were born outside of Canada, in countries diverse as Belgium, Norway, Jamaica, Newfoundland and the United States. In Row C Grave 10 is buried Sergeant John Dick of Shoal Lake, Manitoba. He was killed at Cambrai, October 1st, 1918. He was one of 3 sons of Minnie Dick, all of whom were killed in the Great War. The unknown Sergeant of the Princess Patricia's Canadian Light Infantry buried in Row B Grave 9 is Sergeant George Thompson killed in action September 28th 1918. He is currently commemorated on the Vimy Memorial to the Missing.

RAILLENCOURT COMMUNAL CEMETERY EXTENSION

The cemetery is located east of the village which is 3 kms north-west of Cambrai on the main Arras-Cambrai road. It was made by the Canadian Corps in October 1918. In 1923 another small Canadian cemetery was concentrated into the cemetery.

It now contains the graves of 199 Commonwealth soldiers of which 188 are Canadian (6 are unidentified). The burials are representative of the fierce resistance and heavy casualties suffered by the 3rd Division in their attack on Cambrai. The 1st Mounted Rifles

(Saskatchewan) suffered severely during their attack on the suburbs of Cambrai 29th September 1918.

ST. OLLE BRITISH CEMETERY, Raillencourt

The cemetery is located 500 metres south of the village, which is 3 kms north-west of Cambrai on the main Arras-Cambrai road. It was made by the Canadian Corps Burial Officer in October 1918.

It contains 97 Canadian soldiers (1 is unidentified). 73 of the burials are those of the 116th Battalion (Ontario County) killed 29th-30th September 1918.

Similar to Raillencourt Communal Cemetery Extension and Drummond Cemetery, St. Olle reflects the severe resistance the 3rd Division encountered on the outskirts of Cambrai and the cost to overcome it.

DRUMMOND CEMETERY, Raillencourt

The cemetery is located 2 kms east of the village which is 3 kms north-west of Cambrai on the main Arras-Cambrai Road. It was made by the Canadian Corps Burial officer in October 1918.

It contains the graves of 88 Commonwealth soldiers of which 79 are Canadian (1 is unidentified). The cemetery contains the burials of men of the 3rd Division killed on the outskirts of Cambrai, 28th-30th September 1918. The men of the 2nd Canadian Mounted Rifles (British Columbia), killed 29th September 1918 are in the majority.

CHAPEL CORNER CEMETERY, Sauchy-Lestree

The cemetery is located 1 km south-east of the village, which is located 8 kms north-west of Cambrai, about 2 kms north of the main Arras-Cambrai Road. It was made by fighting units in October 1918 and enlarged by 128 graves by battlefield clearances after the war.

It contains the graves of 178 Commonwealth soldiers of which 62 are Canadian (17 are unknown). The Canadian graves reflect the attack of the 1st Division after clearing the Canal du Nord defences and sweeping north-east towards the Marcoing line. The battlefield clearance brought in many Canadian graves from the Battle of the Drocourt-Queant line, 2nd-3rd September 1918.

In all probability Captain Reginald Bateman of the 46th Battalion (Saskatchewan) is buried here. He was the first professor of English

The grave of Manuel Bermudez in Sancourt British Cemetery. Bermudez was killed in action October 1st 1918 near Bantigny in the Battle of Cambrai. He was born in Venezuela, the son of Manuel Bermudez Lecuna and Carlotta Valdez de Bermudez. He was 24. The Personal Inscription at the base of his headstone reads:

A SON OF VENEZUELA
WHO FOUGHT AND DIED
FOR GOD'S JUSTICE ON EARTH

University of Saskatchewan. Bateman was blown to pieces near Recourt on September 3rd 1918 during the Capture of the Drocourt-Queant line. He is commemorated on the Vimy Memorial.

HAYNECOURT BRITISH CEMETERY

The cemetery is located on the south-west edge of the village which is 8 kms north-west of Cambrai. It was made by the Canadian Corps Burial Officer in October 1918.

It contains the graves of 289 Commonwealth soldiers of which 265 are Canadian (6 are unidentified). The cemetery reflects the rapid advance of the 1st Division from the breakthrough on the Canal du Nord and the later fighting attacking the Marcoing line.

CANTIMPRE CANADIAN CEMETERY

The cemetery is located north of Sailly-les-Cambrai in open country, 6 kms north-west of Cambrai. The cemetery was made by the Canadian Corps Burial Officer in October 1918.

It contains the graves of 224 Commonwealth soldiers of which 222 are Canadian (20 are unidentified). The burials reflect the fierce fighting of the 4th Division in their attacks to break the Marcoing line 28th-30th September and the stubborn defence offered by the Germans. Their are many graves of the 75th (Mississauga Horse) Battalion in the cemetery. Amongst those Canadians buried here are Gordon Douse, age 26, and Henry Douse, age 21, sons of J.G. Douse of Lefroy, Ontario. Both were killed on September 29th 1918, trying to break through the German barbed wire entanglements along the Cambrai-Douai road. They are buried in Row E Graves 24 and 27 respectively.

Private Clarence Caldwell, an American serving with the 75th Battalion is buried in Row B Grave 14. Caldwell had previously served in the U.S. Army and fought in the Spanish- American War and Cuba, 1898-99. He was 40 years old.

SANCOURT BRITISH CEMETERY

The cemetery is located north of the village which is 5 kms north-west of Cambrai. The cemetery was made by the Canadian Corps Burial Officer in October 1918.

It contains the graves of 236 Commonwealth soldiers of which

Per Ardua Ad Astra

The region of Northern France and Flanders in Belgium, is the largest grave-yard in the world. Hundreds of small and large cemeteries dot the countryside from the Swiss border to the Belgian coast. They define the battle lines of the First World War. The cemeteries are national in nature and contain soldiers from Britain, Canada, Australia, New Zealand, South Africa, United States, Italy, Russia, Portugal, Belgium, and Germany. Travelling the old battlefields is an emotional experience and it is hard not to get caught up in the tragedy of 80 years ago. Perhaps the saddest sight is the one you find in the Canada Cemetery near Cambrai. There are 264 soldiers buried here. They were Canadians killed in the Battle of Cambrai. But they are not alone. Along the southern wall are buried the Canadian air crew of a Lancaster bomber shot down in 1944. Seeing the errors of the Great War being repeated 30 years later and costing the lives of the sons of the men who fought here in 1918 gives a strikingly powerful sadness. How could this happen again? The men buried here could well have been buried in the same cemetery that their father was buried in.

On the night of June 12/13th, 1944, the Royal Canadian Air Force launched a major bomber raid on the transport centre of Cambrai. Ninety-two Lancasters left England on the raid, only 83 returned. Nine aircraft, including Lancaster #DS 688, from #408 Squadron, did not return. The entire crew was missing and later listed as killed. The men were recovered from the wreckage and buried by the local authorities in Canada Cemetery amongst their countrymen. Typical of the R.C.A.F. the crew were from across Canada.

Flight Lieutenant (Pilot), Francis Thomas Brice. From Chilliwack, British Columbia.
   Age 24.

Pilot Officer (Air Gunner), Elvin George Todd. From Sudbury, Ontario. Age 20.

Flying Officer (Navigator), Albert Glendenning. From Islington, Ontario.
   Age 30.

Pilot Officer (Wireless/ Airgunner), Harry William Wilson. From St.Catharines, Ontario.
   Age 30.

Pilot Officer (Air Gunner), John Albert Bergeron. From Pouce Coupe, British Columbia.
   Age 19.

Flight Officer (Bomb Aimer), Martin John McDonald. From Moose Jaw, Saskatchewan.
   Age 23.

Rudyard Kipling wrote a short poem after his only son was killed in 1915. It applies here.
   If any question why we died,
   Tell them, because our fathers lied.

LEST WE FORGET.

230 are Canadian (20 are unidentified). The burials reflect the failed attack of the 1st Division toward Abancourt (north-east) on 1st October 1918 and the attacks by the 4th Division 29th-30th September 1918 against the Marcoing line.

From this cemetery there is an excellent view of the battlefield of 1st October 1918, as well as towards Bourlon Wood.

This cemetery reflects the proud tradition of the First Canadian Division and the terrible cost of Cambrai, so many dying so close to the end of the war. There are buried in Sancourt 6 soldiers who were decorated for bravery two times or more.

MILL SWITCH CEMETERY, Tilloy-les-Cambrai

The cemetery is located 3 kms north of Cambrai on the main road from Cambrai to Douai, just north of the motorway overpass. It was made by the Canadian Corps Burial Officer on the German switch line running from the railway embankment to a mill, 330 metres north-west of the cemetery, in October 1918. In 1924 another small Canadian Battlefield Cemetery, Cameron Cemetery, was concentrated into it.

It contains the graves of 107 Canadians (6 are not identified). The cemetery reflects the difficulty encountered by the 3rd Division against uncut barbed wire and German machine guns along the Cambrai-Douai road, 29th September to 1st October 1918.

The 2 Highland Battalions of the 3rd Division, the 42nd Battalion (Black Watch of Montreal) and the 43rd Battalion (Cameron Highlanders of Winnipeg) make up the majority of the burials in the cemetery.

Canada Cemetery is visible 1 km east.

CANADA CEMETERY, Tilloy-les-Cambrai

The cemetery is located north of the village which is 3 kms north of Cambrai. The cemetery was made by the Canadian Corps Burial Officer in October 1918.

It contains the graves of 264 Commonwealth soldiers of which 254 are Canadian (20 are unidentified). Along the eastern wall of the cemetery are buried 6 Royal Canadian Air Force air crew killed in the Second World War when their plane was shot down during a raid on Cambrai, June 13th, 1944.

The burials reflect the battles of the 1st, 3rd and 4th Canadian Divisions in their attempt to encircle Cambrai from the north against determined German resistance.

RAMILLES BRITISH CEMETERY

The cemetery is located on the south side of the village, which is 5 kms north-east of Cambrai. The cemetery was made by the Canadian Corps Burial Officer in October 1918 and enlarged after the war.

It contains the graves of 179 Commonwealth of which 75 are Canadian (6 are unidentified). The cemetery reflects the furthest penetration of the Canadian Corps attempts to cut off Cambrai on 1st October 1918 and the attacks to capture Cambrai and push east 9th-11th October 1918.

NAVES COMMUNAL CEMETERY EXTENSION

The cemetery is located south-west of the village, which is 5 kms north-east of Cambrai. The cemetery was made in October 1918 and enlarged by battlefield clearances after the war.

It now contains the graves of 444 Commonwealth soldiers of which 50 are Canadian (9 are unidentified). The Canadian burials reflect virtually all actions and units involved in the Cambrai fighting.

Corporal James McPhie, VC of the Royal Engineers is buried in Plot II Row E Grave 4. McPhie's Victoria Cross was awarded posthumously for bravery at the Sensee Canal, 14th October 1918.

NIAGARA CEMETERY, Iwuy

The cemetery is located 2 kms south-east of the village, which is 8 km north-east of Cambrai. It was made by the Canadian Corps Burial Officer in October 1918.

It contains the graves of 201 Commonwealth soldiers of which 172 are Canadian (2 are unidentified). The burials reflect the attack by the 2nd Canadian Division on 11th October 1918, pushing the Germans eastward and maintaining pressure on the German defensive rearguard.

Lieutenant Wallace Algie, VC, of the 20th Battalion (Central Ontario), is buried in Row C Grave 7. Algie won his Victoria Cross for bravery near Iwuy on 11th October 1918 by fearlessly overcoming German machine gun positions. He was killed in the same action.

By H. Piffard

THE FATAL MESSAGE

The Canadians who were wounded and later died at Casualty Clearing Stations or at hospitals are buried in several cemeteries, but predominantly those listed below.

BUCQUOY ROAD CEMETERY

The cemetery is located north of the village of Boiry-Ste. Rictrude on the road leading from Arras to Amiens (via Bucquoy). It was made by dressing stations and Casualty Clearing Stations which operated in the vicinity and enlarged by concentrations after the war.

It contains the graves of 1,877 Commonwealth soldiers of which 447 are Canadian. All are soldiers who died of wounds received in the Battle of the Canal du Nord and Cambrai.

In the cemetery are 2 plots of British soldiers killed near Arras in May 1940.

DUISANS BRITISH CEMETERY

The cemetery is located 1 km north of the village of Duisans which is 8 kms west of Arras. The cemetery was made by Casualty Clearing Stations situated near Duisans.

It contains the graves of 3,211 Commonwealth soldiers of which 306 are Canadian. The burials in the cemetery predominantly reflect the Canadian actions throughout 1918; holding the line east and south of Arras as well as the battles of 1918.

Lieutenant Colonel Stanley Gardner, CMG, MC, Commander of the 38th Battalion (Eastern Ontario) is buried in Plot VII Row A Grave 85. He died of wounds received at Cambrai, 30th September 1918. He was 37.

AUBIGNY COMMUNAL CEMETERY EXTENSION

The Cemetery is located south of the village, which is just north of the main Arras-St. Pol Road, 20 kms west of Arras. It was made by Casualty Clearing Stations from 1916 to 1918.

It contains the graves of 2,771 Commonwealth soldiers of which 666 are Canadian. The Canadians buried here reflect the actions throughout their stay on the Arras front from 1916, through the battles of Vimy Ridge, Arras and Cambrai 1918.

Private Claude Patrick Nunney, VC, DCM, MM, 38th Battalion (Eastern Ontario) is buried in Plot IV Row B Grave 39. Nunney won

Albert James Knowling
Lieutenant
Princess Patricia's Canadian
Light Infantry

Killed in action September 28,1918.
Born at Bradwardine, Manitoba,
September 25, 1886.
Enlisted at Montreal, Quebec,
September 20, 1915 in the 4th
Universities Company. Served in
France with the P.P.C.L.I. from April
1916. Promoted Lieutenant in
December 1917.
During military operations on
September 28th, 1918, against the
Marcoing line, east of Bourlon Wood
about 8 a.m., he was hit in the chest
by an enemy rifle bullet and died
almost immediately. He is buried in
Ontario Cemetery, Sains-les-
Marquion.

Ernest Gordon Shepherd
Lieutenant
42nd(The Black Watch of
Montreal) Battalion

Killed in action October 1, 1918.
Born at Montreal, Quebec, May 11th,
1879. He was the son of Francis and
Louise Shepherd of Montreal.
Appointed Lieutenant in the 73rd
Battalion in January 1916. Served in
France from August 1916:
transferred to the 42nd Battalion.
On October 1, 1918 during the Battle
of Cambrai, Lieutenant Shepherd was
advancing against German positions
along the Cambrai-Douai railway
embankment, north of Cambrai when
he was instantly killed by the
explosion of an enemy shell. He is
buried in Ontario Cemetery, Sains-
les-Marquion, France.

his Victoria Cross on the night of 1st / 2nd September 1918 near Vis-en-Artois, by greatly assisting in repelling a German counter-attack.

ETAPLES MILITARY CEMETERY

Etaples Military Cemetery is located on the coastal road between Boulogne and Le Treport, 3 kms north of Etaples. It was used throughout the war and contains 10,729 Commonwealth burials, including 1,123 Canadians. This cemetery reflects all major Canadian Battles of the war; Mount Sorrel, The Somme, Vimy, Passchendaele, Amiens, Arras and Cambrai.

Etaples was the major depot base for the British Army on the Western front and was the location of the infamous Bull Ring and the British Army mutiny of 1917.

On May 19th 1918 German Gotha bombers bombed the No.1 Canadian General Hospital killing 66 soldiers including 3 Nursing Sisters. The men killed in the attack are buried in Plots 66, 67 and 68. The Nursing Sisters are buried in Plot 28.

TERLINCTHUN MILITARY CEMETERY, Wimille

The cemetery is located in view of the English Channel 4 km north of Boulogne. It was opened in the summer of 1918 when the existing cemeteries at Boulogne Eastern and Wimereux Communal were filled. It was used by hospitals in the vicinity.

In 1922 when the cemetery was first closed it contained 3,011 burials of which 277 were Canadian. The cemetery is still open for burials and receives the remains recovered in fields and villages even after 80 years.

It now contains the graves of 4338 Commonwealth soldiers of which 316 are Canadian (27 are unidentified).

The last "identified" Canadian burial took place in 1987 when the remains of Private John Willoughby of the Lord Strathcona's Horse were found in Moreuil Wood. He was killed there 30 March 1918.

In 1976 the identified remains (including his pipe) of Private George Coker of the 4th Battalion Canadian Mounted Rifles (Toronto) were found near Vimy. He was killed 21 April 1917.

The Battles of 1918 being as successful as they were meant that better than 90% (I estimate 93%) of the Canadians killed have a known and honoured grave. The names of those who fell at the Canal du Nord, who were obliterated by shell fire or lost in collapsed dugouts are named on the base of the Vimy Memorial.

By C. Harrison

THE EVOLUTION OF THE FIGHTING MAN

THE GREATEST DOGFIGHT OF THE WAR

The performance of the Canadian Corps was brilliant throughout 1917-18. Their success was unparalleled by any other British Army Corps in the period. Canada's fighter pilots were also outstanding. They produced some of the greatest fighter "Aces" of the war. These included Billy Bishop, Raymond Collishaw, Billy Barker, Maclaren, Claxton, McCall, just to name a few. Canadians made up 10 of the highest scoring "Aces" in the war. Three Canadians won the Victoria Cross for bravery in the air; Billy Bishop, Alan McLeod and Billy Barker. Billy Barker was considered to be the greatest flyer of them all. During the war the man from Dauphin, Manitoba shot down 50 enemy aircraft, including 4 on October 27th, 1918. It was for this incredible, solo dogfight that he won his Victoria Cross. The dog-fight was observed by thousands of Canadian soldiers advancing towards Valenciennes. It was a sight few would forget. The aerial com-bat is described in typical laconic fashion in the Squadron's War Diary.

"On 27th October 1918 William Barker observed an enemy two-seater at 21,000 feet N.E. of the Foret du Mormal. Enemy Aircraft climbed east and Major Barker followed, firing a short burst from underneath at point blank range. E.A. broke up in the air and one of the occupants went out with a parachute. He then observed a Fokker biplane 1,000 feet below stalling and shooting up at him, one of the bullets wounding him in the right thigh. He fell into a spin from which he pulled out in the middle of a formation of about fifteen Fokkers two of which he attacked indecisively, both E.A. spinning down. He turned and getting on the tail of a third which was attack-ing him, shot it down in flames from within ten yards range. At the moment he was again wounded in the left thigh by others of the for-mation who were diving at him. He fainted and fell out of control again. On recovering, he pulled his machine out and was immedi-ately attacked by another large formation of between twelve and fifteen E.A. He at this moment received a third wound from the remainder of the formation who were attacking him. The bullet shat-tered his left elbow. He again fainted and fell out of control to 12,000 feet and, recovering, was at once attacked by another large forma-tion of E.A. He then noticed heavy smoke coming from his machine and under the impression he was on fire, tried to ram a Fokker just ahead of him. He opened fire on it from two to three yards range

Major William G. Barker, V.C.

and the E.A. fell in flames. He then dived to within a few thousand feet of the ground and began to fly towards our lines but found his retreat cut off by another formation of eight E.A. who attacked him. He fired a few bursts at some of them and shaking them off, dived down and returned to our lines a few feet above the ground, finally crashing close to one of our balloons."

He had taken on about sixty enemy aircraft and shot down 4. Barker survived the war and joined the new Canadian Air Force in 1922. He was killed in a plane crash at Ottawa, March 12th, 1930.

Boys will be boys. Six members of the 161st Hurons Own Battalion ham it up in training (1916). They would have a long wait before seeing action in the Spring of 1918. Only in action for 7 months 2 would be killed and 2 others wounded. Cecil Dilling (second from top) and Clare Westcott (second from bottom) were killed. The head of Arnold Westcott (wounded) is third from the top.

THE WESTCOTT TWINS OF SEAFORTH, ONTARIO.

Arnold and Clarence Westcott were born in Seaforth, Ontario on July 30th 1895. Like most identical twins they were inseparable through school and church and in serving their country in the First World War. They enlisted at Seaforth in the 161st Battalion in 1916, obtaining consecutive Regimental Numbers. With many of their friends, the Westcotts trained in Camp Borden, enjoying the soldier's life. They shipped overseas in 1917 and their unit was placed in the 5th Canadian Division in England. They remained there until the 5th Division was broken up for reinforcements in 1918 and sent piece-meal to fighting Battalions in France. In March 1918 both Clare and Arnold joined the 47th Battalion. The 47th was a fighting battalion and fought with the 10th Brigade of the 4th Canadian Division in France and Flanders since 1916.

On April 29th Arnold was severely wounded in the arm and head and evacuated to England. Clare stayed at the Front and fought in the Battles of Amiens and at the Drocourt-Queant line. The unit had not suffered heavily in these battles as many of the other battalions of the 4th Division had. In the Battle of Cambrai the 47th was given the task of leap-frogging the 72nd Battalion and capturing the Marcoing line at Raillencourt. On September 29th 1918 Clarence Westcott was killed in action near Sailly. He was 23. Arnold was notified on October 5th that his twin had been killed. On October 9th 1918 Mrs. Annie Westcott of Seaforth received the following Telegram:

From Ottawa Oct. 9. 18

Mrs Annie Westcott.
    Seaforth
Deeply regret inform you Pte Clarence Charles Victor Westcott infantry officially reported killed in action Sept 29th.

Director of Records

Both boys had kept diaries throughout the war but Clare's 1918 diary had gone missing. In 1919 the diary showed up in Seaforth courtesy of a thoughtful young Canadian soldier who had found it on the field of Battle. He enclosed a touching letter to the grieving mother.

Belgium,
Feb.12,1919

My Dear Mrs. Westcott,

It was only a few days ago I received word that presumably your son, Clarence had been killed in action and I wish to extend to you my deepest sympathy on your sad bereavement.

While advancing over the shell torn area N.West of Cambria with our own Brigade which was relieving, I picked up this diary. Noticing that the Regimental No. in it was one of the 161st from my own home Co. I retained it hoping that some day it might be restored to its rightful owner.

Evidently this portion of the field had been stormed by a platoon of the 47th Battalion consisting mostly of the 161st Huron's Own Boys, who carried ever forward by that indomitable spirit, pushed back, trampling underfoot the accursed Hun who for more than three years had threatened the Civilized World.

This was the courage which completely routed the Huns and resulted in one of the greatest victories ever attained. A victory which will go down in the annals of history as the grandest and most glorious achievement of the Canadian Corps.

May the Almighty sustain and comfort you at this sad hour.
sincerely,

John M. Graham
#528764.
12th Canadian Field Ambulance
France.

Clare Westcott is buried in Anneux British Cemetery, France. Arnold died in 1961.

MUTINY

No one had anticipated the War would end in 1918. The Generals and the Politicians all had made plans for the advance in 1919. So when the German Army collapsed on the Western Front and revolution and rioting in Germany forced the Kaiser to abdicate, and the Germans sued for Peace, the Allies were caught off guard.

One of the major problems facing the Politicians and Generals were what to do with the hundreds of thousands of soldiers no longer required.

For some time plans had been made to demobilize the troops but before the system could be tested it would have to be implemented. Initially demobilization was to be done on a "first over, first back" principal, but as the 1st and 2nd Divisions were in Germany as Occupation forces and the 3rd and 4th Divisions were on Garrison duty in Belgium that principal would be hard to maintain. In England there were thousands of Canadian soldiers, reservists, Corps troops, convalescing soldiers and these were to be the ones to go home first.

The transport logistics of getting these men home were immense and initial calculations of sending home 50,000 men a month were unrealistic and only 25,000 could actually be achieved. In the meantime the Canadians were sitting around in six camps in the United Kingdom waiting.

The boredom, poor pay, cold weather, overcrowding and postponements of the transports caused a significant amount of agitation amongst the troops. The authorities were also aware of "The Red Scare," the rise of Bolshevism and general labour and social unrest throughout Europe. However they did little to placate the men.

The handling of soldiers by some of their officers also created more acrimony. Many officers insisted on the Military "Bull" and this added tension and finally resulted in a strike by the men of the 3rd Division in Belgium. It was only one of 13 strikes by the waiting and impatient Canadian Army. The largest took place at Kinmel Park in Wales. The camp held 19,000 Canadian troops from a variety of units. They became bored and agitated by the cancellation of sailings and the gouging by local merchants at the aptly named "Tintown."

On March 4th, 1919 the men refused to parade after one troopship sailing had been cancelled three times. Finally the tension boiled

The grave of Private Gillan in St. Margaret's Churchyard, Wales. The inscription reads: "In proud memory of Private David Gillan, Aged 22 years, of Florence, Cape Breton, Canada. Who was killed at Kinmel Park on March 5th, 1919 defending the honour of his country."

(PHOTO: N. CHRISTIE)

over and 500 men went on a rampage, looting and destroying the stores in "Tintown." The riot spread through the camp with the men breaking into "wet" canteens, and the Quartermaster's stores. All night and day many of the men fought with other Canadian soldiers who were guarding the camp. Cavalry were used to quell the riot but even they were driven back by a barrage of rocks. A Red Banner was seen amongst the rioters and visions of the Bolshevik menace abounded. Some firing was heard but it appeared to be the Guards who were doing it. The Guards waded into the men, clubbing them with truncheons and using bayonets. When the Kinmel Park riot was over, 11 shops had been looted, the Quartermaster's stores had been looted and 11 canteens had been emptied. For all the rioting only 28 men had been wounded, mostly broken limbs and bruises. But 5 men were dead. One was a Russian rioter, William Tarasevitch who had been bayonetted when attacking an officer. David Gillan, a guard had been shot, as had William Haney and Jack Hickman. No one knew for sure who had done the shooting. The fifth man, Corporal Joseph Young, who had served in France since 1916 had died as well, but the circumstances of his death were unknown even to the authorities.

On March 6th, 1919 General Sir Richard Turner, V.C. visited the camp and yielded to many of the rioters' requests. They received an advance of pay, partial amnesty and a promise of more sailings. The authorities blamed the riot on the influence of Bolsheviks and French Canadiens. Their claims were completely unfounded but they were the scapegoats of the period.

An inquest was held and 51 men were Court-Martialled. Many were acquitted but those who appeared as "Reds" or those who just happened to be born in Eastern Europe received the heaviest sentences of between 5 and 10 years penal servitude. No one was tried for the deaths of Tarasevitch, Young, Gillan, Haney or Hickman[9].

By June, 1919 the vast majority of the Canadians had returned home and were discharged. The War was over.

---

[9] The remains of John Frederick Hickman were repatriated and he is buried in Dorchester, New Brunswick. He was 21. The other four rest in St. Margaret's Churchyard, Bodelwydden, Wales.

THE SPANISH FLU

Frederick Bateman was born on February 7th, 1890 inPickering, Ontario. Frederick Lloyd Bateman was the son of Richard Bateman, M.D. and Mary Bateman of Danforth Avenue, Toronto. He was educated at Pickering Quaker College and later at the Whitby Collegiate Institute. In 1907 he joined the Canadian Bank of Commerce in Montreal as a bank clerk. Like most men of his age he joined the Colours in May 1916, enlisting in the 6th McGill Seige Battery, Canadian Garrison Artillery.

In early 1917 Fred Bateman went overseas and fought with his unit at Vimy, Passchendaele, Amiens, Arras and Cambrai. During this period he was gassed twice. After the Armistice he went with the 4th Canadian Division to Brussels as part of a major Garrison force. Greatly relieved to have survived the war, Fred Bateman waited for his turn to return home.

But Europe was still a dangerous place. The First World War had cost roughly 20 million lives, but at the end of 1918 a plague swept Europe. For the first time since the middle ages Europeans were dying, defencelessly, in the face of the Spanish Influenza epidemic. It attacked all ages and killed rapidly, by weakening the defence systems and allowing pneumonia to take hold and kill. Canadian soldiers were readily susceptible to the virus and many who had survived the dangers and horrors of the battlefields succumbed to the Spanish flu. Maybe the soldiers had been weakened by the years in the trenches or perhaps emotional exhaustion set-in after the Armistice, but throughout Europe many Canadian soldiers died.

Returning soldiers brought the Spanish flu with them and more than 50,000 Canadians from across Canada became victims of the influenza epidemic. The Canadian Government was deeply disturbed by the flu and banned public gatherings and even tried to postpone the Armistice celebrations. The Stanley Cup competition was cancelled in 1919. The epidemic finally ended by the end of 1919 but it had killed an estimated 20 million people, world-wide.

Fred Bateman contracted the flu after the Armistice. Weakened by the flu, he developed pneumonia and died in Brussels on December 11th, 1918. He is buried in Brussels Town Cemetery with 40 other Canadian soldiers who had survived the Great European War, only to fall to another European affliction.

MONS, THE END OF THE WAR.

The last act of the Great War was to bury the last of the fallen. Canada had lost 34 men killed and 23 soldiers wounded on November 10th, 1918. One Canadian soldier was killed on November 11th, 1918. In a show of respect the citizens of Mons collected together the Canadians who died there and with the utmost reverence laid them to rest in Mons Cemetery. What transpired is best described in the Official History of the 42nd Battalion, The Black Watch of Canada.

"No casualties of any description were suffered by the 42nd Battalion on November 11th and the total casualties on November 10th were 6 other ranks killed and 1 officer and 24 other ranks wounded. All of these occurred before the evening of the 10th and 12 of them, including 2 men killed, took place in the Transport lines at Jemappes due to shelling of the back area. Moreover, there was a curious and most noticeable contrast in the demeanour of the troops and that of the civil population in Mons on Armistice Day. There was, to the troops, a sense of unreality about it all and it is often a matter of comment among those who were present that it was several days before full appreciation of the fact that hostilities had ceased came home to them.

On November 12th the funeral of Lance-Corporal Jones, Private Mills, Private Daigle and Private Brigden, together with several members of other Canadian units who had been killed outside the city, took place in Mons. The Municipal Council asked permission of the Divisional Commander that the citizens of Mons be allowed to honour the dead by a public service. This permission was granted and a most elaborate and memorable funeral service was arranged. "With the most reverent and loving care," runs the record, "the Civic Authorities made all preparations. A room in the old City Hall was draped in black and silver and there the caskets were laid out in state from 10 o'clock in the morning until 2 in the afternoon, while a great throng of people paid their tributes and heaped the room with wreaths and flowers. The funeral cortege was comprised of representatives of every, rank and class; practically the entire city followed to the graves. In the great multitude one little group commanded our especial respect, the veterans of the Franco-Prussian war, old men in

Fred Meikle Pulford
Captain
27th (City of Winnipeg) Battalion

Killed in action October 1, 1918.

Born at Winnipeg, Manitoba, October 3rd, 1891. He was the son of Walter and H.E. Pulford of Winnipeg.

In October 1914 he enlisted in the 27th Battalion. He served in France from September 1915 and was promoted to Captain.

On October 1, 1918, Pulford was at the Battalion H.Q., situated in a sunken road near Tilloy. The H.Q. was shelled and at 12:30 p.m., an enemy shell burst behind him and he was hit in the head and instantly killed by a large shell fragment. Buried in Bourlon Wood Cemetery, France.

Frederick John Longworth
Lieutenant
Canadian Field Artillery

Died of wounds November 10,1918

Born in Charlottetown, Prince Edward Island, September 21, 1893. Son of Louise and John Longworth of Charlottetown.

Appointed Lieutenant in May 1915; wounded August 31, 1917; awarded the Military Cross for bravery.

On the afternoon of November 10, 1918 he was in charge of his battery near Mons when an enemy high-explosive shell burst at his feet severing both his legs above the knee. He was taken to a house in Jemappes and was attended to by a Medical Officer but died 30 minutes later. Longworth is buried in Jemappes Communal Cemetery, Belgium.

faded uniforms with forgotten decorations on their breasts. There was something both pathetic and heroic in their enfeebled ranks as they marched with the men of a new day and another race.

The old cemetery at Mons is situated on a little wooded hill looking to the West and among the quiet trees we gathered about the open graves. The service was conducted by Major the Reverend G. G. D. Kilpatrick, then Divisional Chaplain. Prayer was offered, a few verses of Scripture read, a few words spoken and then the crackling volleys of the Firing Party rang out above us as the sun went down, golden with its promise of another dawn and radiant with the message of the day that shall not die and the life eternal beyond the margin of this world; the silver notes of the bugle sent out the call of the Last Post- 'Come home, Come home.' So we left them, our honoured dead."

The funeral orations of the representative of the City of Mons and the Parliamentary representative of the Province of Hainaut, delivered with a ringing sincerity that moved hundreds of those in the great assemblage to tears, illustrate the depth of the feeling of the civil population of Mons:-

"Gentlemen, The representative of the City of Mons makes his salutation before the graves of those who have watered with their blood the remnant of Belgian soil which they swore to deliver from tyranny; he comes in the name of the people of Mons to salute those who sacrificed their lives in advance to the cause of outraged right, and who, coming from afar, after months and years of ceaseless fighting, when just reaching the end which would reward all their trying labour, have fallen on the field of honour, covered with glory."

"Alas, many of these brave men rest in our Belgian soil, since the first we saw coming to oppose its invasion as the indignant protest of British loyalty against German rapine; since those who first fough at the side of our men in the mud of the Yser around Ypres, holding back the rising tide of Huns; until the time of those who in devastate France have lately fallen in such numbers at Quievrain; and now the that we lay in the ground of our ancestors to-day, to sleep in pea beside so many that we have loved."

"Their noble and brilliant example illumines the world and serve as a beacon-light to coming generations. The glory in wl a they have arrayed themselves radiates to-day; and with how much uffering, with how much effort, with how much sorrow, have they paid for it!"

"In the glory of victory, before the halo which encircles reestablished right, amidst the joy of triumph, we must turn to look upon those who died fighting as a simple duty amongst all the horrors of this frightful war. This calms our minds to think quietly, almost on our knees, of those Canadian heroes who fell before Mons in delivering it from the Germans, on the very threshold of the final reward."

"The entire British world has determined to keep its word as given by England, noble Canada has shed rivers of blood, Belgium is free and civilization is saved."

"To accomplish this, it was necessary, after Belgium had rejected with dignity the disgraceful offers of a criminal Kaiser, after she had been bespattered with every insult, after she had undergone a martyr's suffering, it was necessary that from afar, brothers we knew not should come to us to strive beside us, to give their lives for us. Glory be to them!"

It was Mons that saw the first soldiers of the British Army arrive in August, 1914, and Mons received its Canadian deliverers at the moment when the Huns were asking for grace and mercy. Mons will perpetuate their memory in stone and bronze, but more durable still will be the reverence that every father will hand down to his son, every mother to her child, in the years to come, and all those who have had the privilege of seeing these hours of glory and heroism will never forget who it is to whom all their splendour is owing; and for centuries to come the name of Canada will stand connected here with the very words Honour, Loyalty and Heroism.

"So we beg of you, gentlemen, to take home with you our heartfelt and unending gratitude."

The Deputy of the Province of Hainaut then spoke, saying:

"General and Gentlemen, May I be allowed to add to the touching words of the representative of the City of Mons, a tribute of respect from the whole population of the Province of Hainaut to the memory of the brave men whose mortal remains will now be laid in ground which is free again at last, freed by their courage and their sacrifice."

"Before these graves which await them, emotions arise which go to the heart, and thoughts which dominate the mind. The life of a man, flashing out between two eternities, takes its significance and its value not from the number of years that it may last, but from what it contains in noble aspirations and unselfish acts. There are hours that within their sixty minutes are more exalted and more productive than the sixty years of an existence devoid of ideal. He it is that has truly lived, he it is that truly lives after his death, who had known how to leave in his passage through this world an act deeply imprinted on the heart, be it only of one of his comrades, as a mark of gratitude and affectionate remembrance.

"Such was the life of those that their brothers in arms now lay to rest amongst those whom we have loved and whom we always love, that their remembrance may be blended.

"Gentlemen of the Canadian Corps, We bow, filled with respect and deep feeling before the tomb of your comrades. In so doing, we enshrine in our hearts the remembrance of what they were and of what they have done for us, that we may hand it down to our children and to the grandchildren of our children, as the choicest of heirlooms.

"At this moment, alas! afar, beyond the Atlantic, there are mothers and fathers, wives and children, lovers, brothers, sisters, that await those who live no longer, not knowing as yet that they lie here. I feel that there arises from our hearts, to fly across the ocean, a warm and brotherly sympathy. We press to our grateful hearts all those families that we have become acquainted with through the heroism of their sons. May God grant that they may feel the comfort of this sympathy, before the sad news reaches them.

"Tell them, we beg of you, that this little remnant of Belgian soil is for us the most sacred of all; that it is a part of Canadian territory, a priceless treasure set like a jewel in the burial ground of our own people; priceless because it embraces the remains of noble sons of Canada

"Our heads bow before their tombs, but our hearts, proud of having been defended by them, gather forever around them to become faithful guardians of the sacred repose of your Brothers in Arms."

So ended the Great War.

FOR FURTHER REFERENCE

This book has dealt solely with the attack on the Canal du Nord and Cambrai made by the Canadians in September-October 1918. The attacks of September-October 1918 extended along the length of the Hindenburg line and involved many British, Australian, New Zealand and American units.

There is also much else to see on the Great War Battlefields and I have listed below a number of excellent references to the battlefields of the First World War.

References to the "Advance to Victory" or the "Last Hundred Days" are few and far between. There are a few memorials, but visitors usually visit the main battlefields of Ypres and the Somme. When the "The Last Hundred Days" are mentioned it is almost in passing, as if the whole thing was like a knife cutting through butter. This is a shame for these men fought an ever tough German opponent and captured defensive positions that would have taken their predecessors of 1915, 1916 or 1917 months, if at all.

However, I have listed books which can shed some light on the final victories:

Battle Guides

Before Endeavours Fade, by R.E. Coombs. Battle of Britain Prints International, 1976.

The Somme Battlefields, by M. And M. Middlebrook. Viking 1981.

The Somme Then and Now, by J. Giles. Battle of Britain Prints International, 1986.

The Western Front, Then and Now, by J. Giles. Battle of Britain Prints, 1992.

Australian Battlefields of the Western Front, by J. Laffin. Kangaroo Press, 1992.

The Advance to Victory

The Official History of the Canadian Expeditionary Force 1914-19, by G.W.L. Nicholson. The Queen's Printer, 1962.

Canada's Hundred Days, by J.F.B. Livesay. Thomas Allen, 1919.

Spearhead to Victory, by D. Dancocks. Hurtig Publishers, 1987.

A Wood Called Bourlon, by William Moore. Leo Cooper, 1988.

With the Canadian Army Medical Corps in the Last Hundred Days, by A.E. Snell. F.A. Ackland 1924.

A MAN FROM MOOSEJAW TALKS ON TRENCH COATS

H_E butted into the billet and the middle of the conversation after the joyous manner of his kind.

" What's that about coats ? " he said, kicking fragments of France from his clodded boots.

" There's only one trench coat that ever gets itself outside of me now, henceforth and for ever, and that's the " Thresher."   Boys, the man that put me wise to this immaculate conception of a field habilament was the good Samaritan in the 1918 edition and a Sam Browne belt.   He was the main guy of the ancient order of true friends—and then some.   The hot air required to tell what he didn't know about kit and campaigning wouldn't inflate a two-cent balloon.

" Well, here's the coat, and I'd like you perambulating mud-pies to notice the quantity of prime Picardy that *hasn't* stuck to it.   Why the things some of you call trench-coats have got an appetite for mud like a goat for gum boots.   The trenches get half an inch wider every time you walk through 'em.   Give me 10 cents and I'll buy back all the mud you can scrape off this coat at 5 dollars an ounce.   And protection !   I've never seen rain work harder to get through a garment than it has done for the last twelve hours—but this old " Thresher " didn't even notice it.

" And, say, when you're talking about warm coats there's just one remark I'd like to chip in with—the man who can raise a shiver in this coat would catch cold in hell.   And *that* isn't all there is to the " Thresher."   The fellow who worked out these neck and wrist dodges was some brain merchant.   When you're upholstered in a " Thresher," my sons, you're the giddiest kind of top-hole trench furniture that ever lived on lyddite."

The THRESHER

The Thresher Trench Coat, with detachable Kamelcott lining - - -	£7 7 0
The Thresher Trench Coat, unlined - -	£5 5 0
Detachable Sheepskin Lining, extra - -	£4 4 0
Cavalry pattern, with knee flaps and gusset, extra - - - - -	£1 1 0

Send size of chest and approximate height when ordering.

THRESHER & GLENNY
(E_{STABLISHED} 1755)

—— *Military Tailors and Outfitters,* ——

152 & 153 STRAND, LONDON, W.C.2

By Appointment to  H.M. The King

KIT IN GENERAL.
Generations have known Thresher Kit as top value at bottom price— as, for instance :
Whipcord Field Service Jackets, 115/-, 126/-, and 136/6
Slacks, Whipcord, 42/-, 55/- and 57/6
Bedford Cord Riding Breeches, 63/- and 84/-
British Warm, Camel Vicuna, 126/-
Folder X with full range of prices and self-measurement form free on request.

Thresher & Glenny accept all risks as to kit with customers' own measures if taken in accordance with the form sent.

Contemorary advertisement. The Great war was a great opportunity for many merchants to get rich.